Smashing Through The Stop Sign Of Life

True life-changing experiences of mental health, dreams, shocks, cancer & hurdles leading to strength, power, and positivity

RA

Compilation of 17 International Authors
Copyright © 2021. Rebecca Adams. All Rights Reserved

SMASHING THROUGH THE STOP SIGN OF LIFE

Copyright © 2021 compiled by Rebecca Adams

All rights reserved. Published in the United Kingdom. No part of this book may be used or reproduced mechanically, electronically, or by any other means, including photocopying, without prior written consent of the author. It is illegal to copy this post to a website or distribute it by any other means without permission from the Author.
This is a work of non-fiction. No names have been changed, no characters invented, no events fabricated. All co-authors are accountable for their chapters inside this book.

For information contact :

www.rebeccaadamsbiz.com

Published by Rebecca Adams Publishing House

Book and Cover design by Rebecca Adams

Cover Illustration & Images by Phoebe Adams

ISBN (paperback): 979-8-47995-229-6
ASIN (kindle/ebook) : B09HMY7MBB

First Edition : October 2021

10 9 8 7 6 5 4 3 2 1

Smashing Through The Stop Sign Of Life

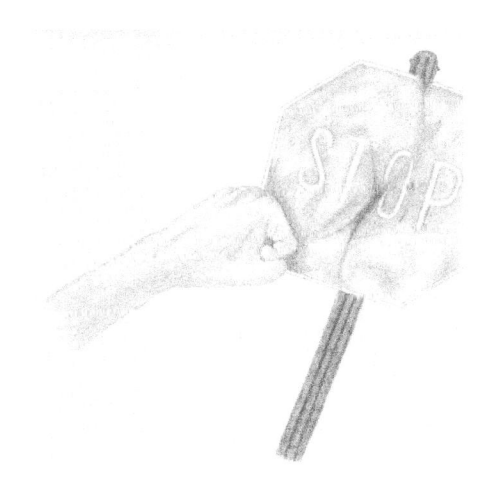

"Smash Through your own Stop Sign of Life"

Rebecca Adams

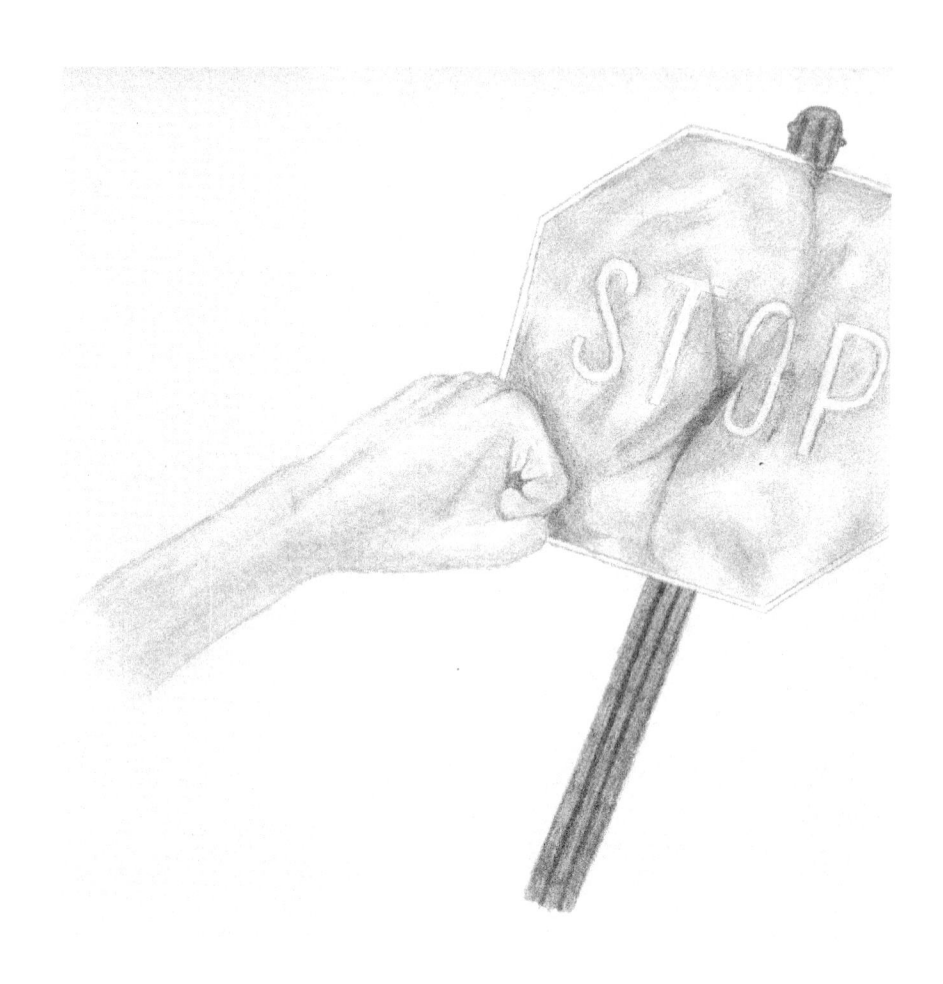

Dedication

I dedicate this book, to you, the reader. I am so grateful that you are holding this book in your hands and are ready to read it. I want you to know that you are supported and please do not feel like you are alone, because you aren't. Reach out to any co-author in this book and connect with them.

Do know that you are an incredible human being, and that no matter what you have been through or are going through – you most definitely can come through to the other side bigger, better, bolder, wiser, and stronger than ever before.

It's okay to feel down at times. It's okay to take a break and rest. It's okay to be quiet and submerse into doing your inner work. Concentrate on your mindset daily and you'll start to see a difference in the way that you are, the way you feel and respond.

Know that life is always moving forwards, things will always be changing, (like the seasons do) and know that you have a part to play whilst you're here on earth. You matter and you are significant.

Please read this book and connect with me about your thoughts. I encourage you to work through any emotions you may have by writing in a journal to help release anything that may show up for you.

Thank you for being here. We all appreciate you.

Warmest wishes,
Rebecca.x

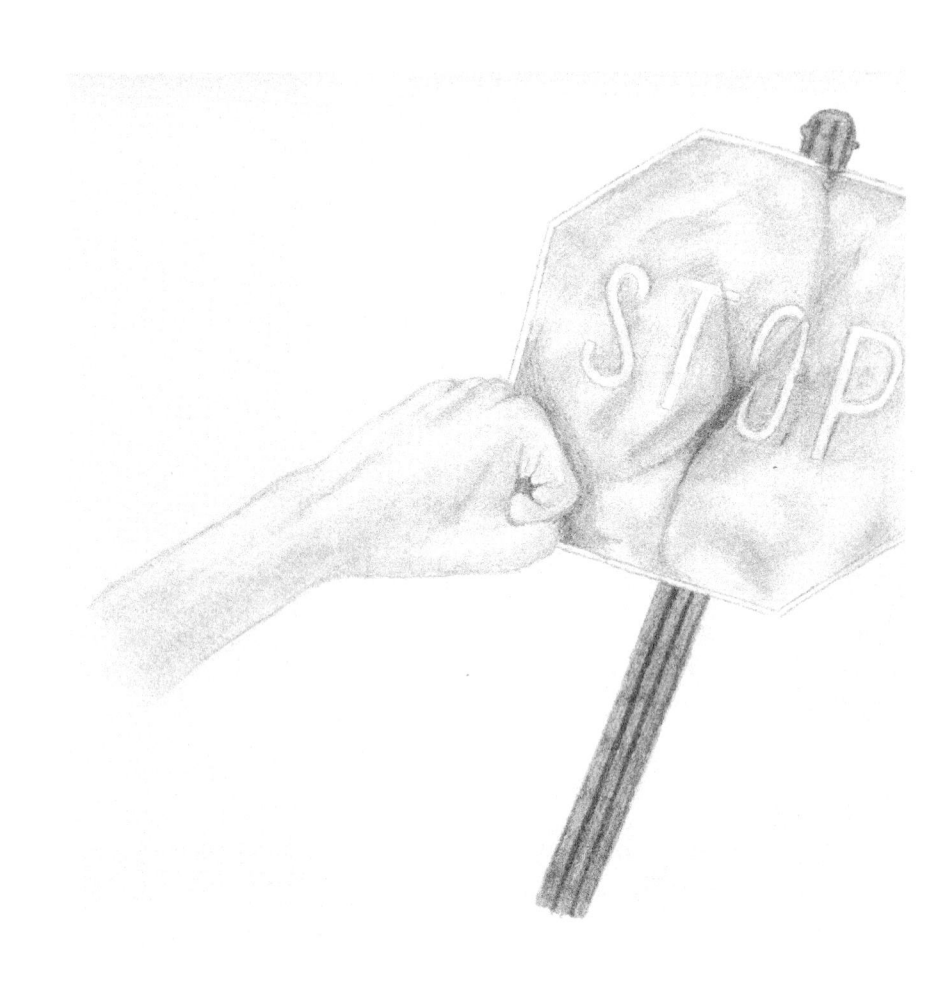

Foreword

I was honoured, humbled and excited when Rebecca asked me to write the foreword of this incredible book Smashing Through the Stop Sign of Life (the final book in the Smashing Through trilogy). This book depicts the journey of the human struggle of abuse, depression, despair, and loss.

Seventeen authors from around the world unite to share real-life stories that they have lived through. You will connect at the soul level to the suffering and pain they endured. Each author shares how they discovered their own inner greatness and how they were able to move through their ordeal and come out the other side as winners.

Their heartfelt stories will take you on an emotional journey where you will witness the resilience of the human soul. You will find yourself and your own story within this page-turning book. It is a book that you will want to pick up and read again and again throughout your life. You will want to share this book with loved ones who may be going through a tough time.

This book is an encyclopaedia of powerful stories on overcoming life's adversities and coming out the other side triumphant. The authors have poured their heart and soul into their chapter Some sharing their story for the very first time, deciding it's time to make a difference and touch lives.
Our modern world is forever changing, but the journey and struggles of the soul remain the same.

"Smashing Through the Stop Sign of Life" reminds us that life's challenges do not have to break us down but offers us a breakthrough to the greater part of ourselves and to smash through adversities that life throws at us.

This life-changing book will leave you feeling uplifted, empowered, and motivated to make changes in your own life. You will feel encouraged to find your inner strength and smash through the stop sign in your life.

Imani Speaks

www.imanispeaks.com

CONTENTS

SMASHING THROUGH THE STOP SIGN OF LIFE I
SMASHING THROUGH THE STOP SIGN OF LIFE III
"SMASH THROUGH YOUR OWN STOP SIGN OF LIFE" V
DEDICATION VII
FOREWORD IX
CONTENTS 1
"REMEMBER YOU'RE WORTH MORE THAN RUBIES &
DIAMONDS" 1
REBECCA ADAMS 1
INTRODUCTION 1
.... 5
KEEP GOING ALWAYS™ 7
CONSCIOUS STATE: SWITCHING REALITY 21
A ROUTINE VISIT TO THE DR'S CHANGED EVERYTHING 33
THEY MAY HAVE PULLED THE PLUG BUT THEY'LL NEVER
SWITCH US OFF 47
THE POWER OF THE WHISPER IN YOUR SOUL 63
THE GIFT OF DANCE 75

HOW MANY HURDLES DOES ONE HAVE TO TAKE?	89
LETTER THROUGH THE POST	103
MY JOURNEY TO MOTHERHOOD	115
NEVER BE AFRAID TO START OVER	127
"JUST HOLD MY HAND – WE WILL BE SAFE"	141
GIVEN A SECOND CHANCE SO GOING TO LIVE IT!	153
TO TELL YOU MY STORY IS TO TELL OF HIM!	165
MARRIED TO THE WRONG ONE!	177
THE PHONE CALL I HAD BEEN DREADING!	189
SMASHING THROUGH YOUR FEAR OF STIGMA	201
CLOSING THOUGHTS	211
ACKNOWLEDGEMENTS OF THE "SMASHING THROUGH' SERIES	213
SPONSORS	219

"Remember You're Worth More Than Rubies & Diamonds"

Rebecca Adams

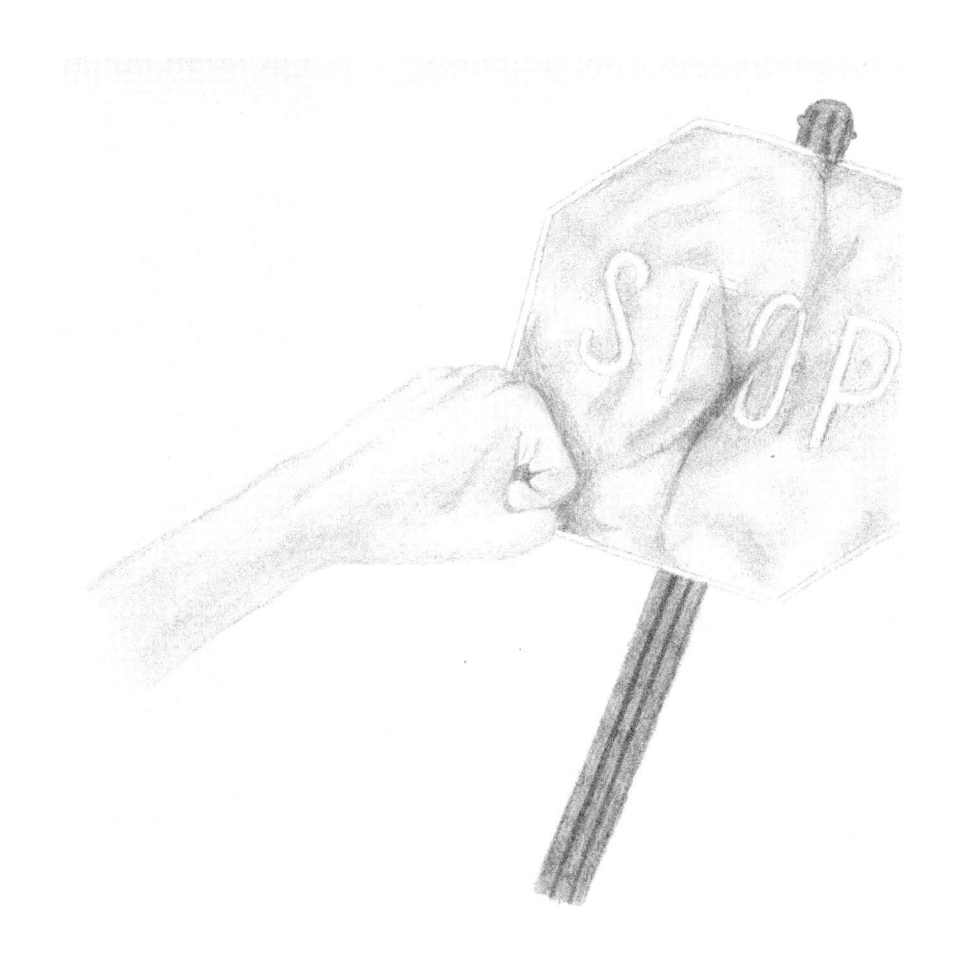

Introduction

I welcome you into this final book of the "Smashing Through…" trilogy series of books. I am very proud of the dedication and commitment from the co-authors in all 3 books.

These books are all designed with you, the reader, in mind. For you to know that no matter what situation you are dealing with or have faced, you are not alone, and you can reach out to get the advice, wisdom and support needed to help you.

In life, things happen. Good and bad, positive and negative and sometimes, damn right awful things, BUT you are not meant for a life of half-hearted fulfilment. You are meant to experience such wonder, amazement, abundance, greatness, and beautiful moments.

You get a chance every single day to wake up and decide how you're going to feel and how you want your day to go. Despite the downsides that may show themselves to you – you can always choose to unlearn, to flourish, to grow, to expand and to be empowered with the knowledge that you are awesome, incredible, enough, worthy, and brilliant.

YES, YOU ARE!

No matter what "STOP SIGN OF YOUR LIFE" is telling you 'NO' or to 'STOP'… you can SMASH THROUGH it to design your life, say enough is enough, say no more and truly take charge and control of what you can.

Life can be full of sadness, BS, upset, anger, panic, fear, and much more icky and negative things… however, it can also be completely full of smiles, jokes, laughter, love, happiness, exploring, abundance, gratitude and peace.

You get to decide. You truly do.

You can smash that "stop sign of life" down with your fist, with your mind, with a hockey stick, with a martial arts kick or with your voice… to give a BIG resounding 'NO' to anyone or anything that's holding you back from accomplishing the best that you want your life to be. You always have choices.

One technique I use, that I'd like to share with you is called EFT (Emotional Freedom Technique), sometimes known as "Tapping". It's a belief clearing technique used by thousands of people around the world to help them release all of the negative emotions and thoughts they have that may be affecting their life. There are many areas on the body that you use to tap on, with your fingers repeatedly, whilst saying certain affirmations and sentences. You can have a look on YouTube for many videos to explain this more and for you to choose what points on your body that are best for you. Mine is the 'karate chop'.

With EFT you get to choose what you say. So, the opening statement is "Even though……." And then you fill in the blank with whatever is going on for you. It could be something that someone said, a situation you're experiencing or a feeling you're having. As you tap on the specific point on your body, you are channelling and tapping out all the negative emotions and thoughts as you are saying the sentences and phrases. Then the ending statement is "I deeply and completely accept myself and how I feel".

An example for you; "Even though {X said that I am not good enough and I'm not worthy. I know that I am amazing, awesome, and strong. That is their opinion, and I don't need to accept that as my truth. I deserve respect, appreciation, and love within all areas of my life. I know this to be true and real. I deeply and completely love and accept myself and how I feel}".

I always concentrate on my breathwork, whilst I am doing my EFT. It helps to create a genuine feeling of peace, grounding, a strong mindset, and control. It is a very strong belief clearing technique that can be used on any area of your life or business. I encourage you to try it and see how you get on. It may be exactly what you need, and it'll work for some people and not for others – that's okay either way

The one thing that I want you to know is that LIFE IS PRECIOUS, and you'll find yourself going through periods in your life of light and dark, flow and ease, moments that are testing and difficult, BUT protect your energy and soul above it all. You need to be devoted to being your own original blueprint and to be yourself, throughout everything whilst you're here on this beautiful planet. Dive deep and find your inner strength, work on your "Lion Mindset" daily and know that you can heal, do what aligns with you and rewrite your future.

Don't ever feel that you have to dim your light. Keep shining brightly and show up to your life – you only get one! Use your strength to share your story with other people, to inspire and motivate them and show them the light too. Be the beacon of hope and light – you never know who you'll empower.

Trust the process. Believe in yourself. Don't compare yourself to anyone and work on yourself more than you do anything else.

Pour into you every single day. Schedule time in for you, even if it's 15 mins, so that you can keep topped up. Strive for happiness, peace, and joy within yourself, by yourself and then when you share your life with others who have done the same, it'll feel even more incredible. It's all about ADDING VALUE and you'll see and feel more contentment.

No matter what you experience in your life, know that you can and will achieve anything you set your mind to. You've got this!

Reach out. Get the support you need and know that you are a king and queen. Remember, you're worth more than rubies and diamonds.
Rebecca.x

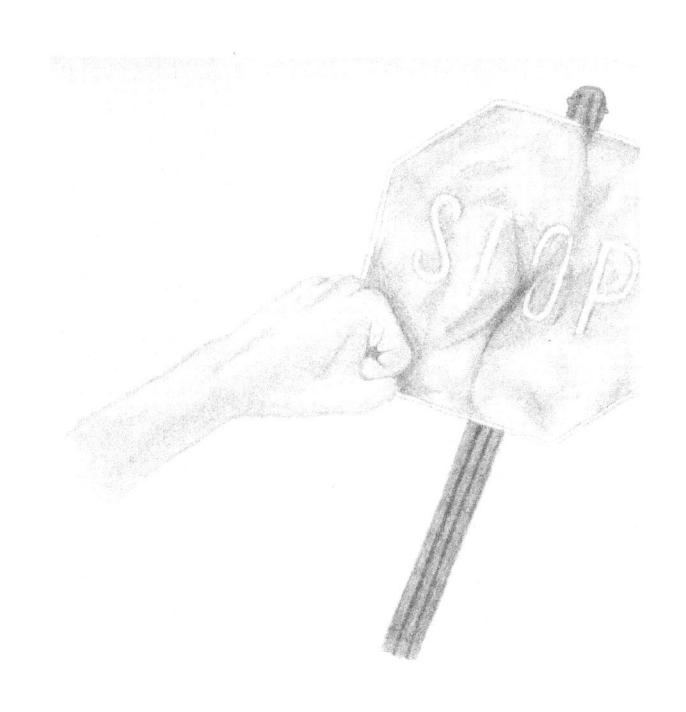

"Mindset is everything. It's like breathing"

Rebecca Adams

Keep Going Always ™

"Have you heard of the word 'AUTISM' before?" Those words came out of the mouth of my son's paediatrician.

It was the year 2000 and my friend, who worked as a nursery nurse, had mentioned to me a few things she had noticed Dominic doing that were concerning. These things, as a first time Mum, I didn't know or pick up on, as I thought every child did them.

Dominic was obsessed with the doors being closed constantly, lining his toy cars up in a row, all facing the same way…but, when one was turned round the opposite way, then all hell would break loose. The same goes for any routines that were changed and also, if any food was touching other food on his plate. Meltdowns galore happened and they weren't pretty. Plus, he did so many other things daily, too many to mention.

My friend recommended that I speak to the health visitor. So I did, and my son was then referred to a paediatrician.

I was quite nervous walking all the way to the health centre with Dominic in his pram for this appointment as I didn't know what to expect. Since my friend had mentioned things to me about Dominic's behaviour and rituals, I was conscious of them and found myself looking out for more and more and taking note. Obviously, the fact that his speech had deteriorated was major and he had stopped saying "Mum".

I sat in the waiting room and waited for his name to be called. A lady came into the room and called his name and so we went into the room whereby the paediatrician did all the necessary checks on Dominic and said that she was also referring him to someone higher than herself. I said "okay".

She walked us out, back into the waiting room and then she asked me the question I will never forget; "Have you heard of the word 'AUTISM' before?". I answered "No" and so she asked me whether I owned a computer and if I had the internet. (Reading this, as I write this in 2021 seems bizarre but back then, not everyone did have access to the world wide web).

"Yes, I do" I answered, and she gave me a website address to look at. As I walked home, bewildered by the appointment, and hearing her question repeatedly in my head, I didn't know what to think. I didn't know the severity of how my life and Dominic's life would change forever!

Dominic was asleep by the time I got back home to my damp 2-bed flat, so I made a coffee and fired up the computer. The screech of the internet dial-up took forever and then I was connected. I typed into the search bar the word AUTISM and let the internet do its thing.

OH, MY WORD!!!! My heart pumped out of my chest, tears streamed down my face as I scrolled and read more and more. My brain couldn't keep up! "THIS CAN'T BE RIGHT?!".

The more I read, the more shocked I was, and it was so overwhelming... it was truly unbelievable. Hours went by and I was still reading, taking notes, and crying.

Ryan rang me and I told him. His calm tone of voice and words to me were "Whether it is autism or not, we'll be fine". With that, I fed my son and put him to bed. I watched him as he slept, so young and little, with not a care in the world.

Now, if you know the Rebecca of 2021 and beyond, you know that the Rebecca from 2000 changed in that moment and so I threw myself into months of research, printing off everything I could and highlighting certain phrases, sentences, and paragraphs. I needed to know as much as I could and what the path may look like. I joined chat groups and messenger groups (no social media existed back then) and I met an amazing lady named Andrea. We started emailing each other and she asked me what Dominic's traits were etc, so I told her, and I always remember the email back to me. My son reminded her of her own who had been diagnosed with Autism. Wow!

I was armed with knowledge, with having an amazing friend in Andrea, (I'm forever grateful to her), who could guide and support me in the right direction and so Dominic and I went to every appointment scheduled in and we were told that the process could take 9mths for the assessment and further for diagnosis too. We were already on the 'Autism Train' so let's go! I didn't care how long it took, at that point, I needed to know – one way or the other.

Back then, on benefits, I couldn't afford PECS (Picture Exchange Communication System) so I decided to have a look at how I could make my own, so I bought a cork board and stuck Velcro on it, that I got from a local sewing shop. I printed off pictures of items on cardboard and attached the sticky Velcro to the back in order to teach Dominic how to communicate with me by handing me a picture of what he wanted. I also used my Polaroid Camera to take photos of the potty, the toilet, the pram, Dominic's toothbrush etc and attach them all to a big keyring that we could carry round in the nappy bag (diaper bag) so that Dominic could communicate with me 'on the move'.

It took constant work with the system I'd made, and months went by before Dominic started to make progress. One day he'd give me the photo of the potty, then he wouldn't. It's as though his brain couldn't remember. I persevered and kept going with it all. Months of momentum and consistency was eventually working, slowly but surely.

I remember Dominic having to see a speech and language therapist to determine whether he needed S.A.L.T and, he couldn't go to nursery anymore as I couldn't drop him off and leave him as they couldn't deal with him. On one occasion I left him, and I was called back within 20mins as he was in a full-blown meltdown screaming and headbutting the tiled floor in the nursery bathroom. I went in, calmed him down and we left after the headteacher said he couldn't return. I understood but that's where the segregation started.

I was cataloguing everything down - what Dominic could and couldn't do, his reactions and everything so when we were called for the final meeting with a very highly qualified doctor, we knew it was "THE day". Everything had been pointing towards Autism. We needed the diagnosis confirmation and we needed it in writing.

Sept 11th, 2001… Ryan and I walked, with Dominic in his pram to the appointment and as I sat in reception, waiting to go in, my hands were sweaty. I was looking for reassurance from Ryan and he said, "It's okay". My son's name was called, and we went into the room.

The doctor did some checks on Dominic, read the paperwork, and then told us the news that "YES, Dominic has Autism".

The sigh of relief, that I wasn't going mad. That I wasn't a 'bad parent' and the entirety of the journey had caught up with me as I cried when we left the room. Every little trait that Dominic had and did – made sense. All of the months and months of research I had done, now came into play even more.

"It's okay, we are okay" – those words repeatedly in my head and we were told that the confirmation letter would be sent to my home and before I could blink, we were walking to my Mum's home.

My Mum, who was a nurse, was at work and Bill (my Mum's husband) was in the living room and told us that the Twin Towers in NYC had been hit by planes. It felt surreal and a completely shocking day. We walked home and put the news on. There it was… lives changed on that day for so many. My heart goes out to everyone affected.

I remember back in 1999, before Dominic's diagnosis, I was walking home from town one day, in the pouring rain, with Dominic in his stroller (rain cover down and fast asleep – not knowing anything that was going on). I was trying to carry all the shopping; push Dominic home, up and down the kerbs and pavements, and I was crying because everything was getting too much. The drivers of the cars going by couldn't tell I was crying as it was raining that bad and I looked like a drowned rat!

All that was going on in my head was that I had no money, no job and so what was I going to do? What was the point in it all? I was tired, frustrated and upset. My self-esteem was low, and I was questioning myself as a Mum and thought I had failed.

I managed to eventually get home, soaked to the skin by the rain, and put all the shopping away whilst Dominic was asleep. In my deepest darkest moment, I knew that something had to change and there was more to life than this. I spoke to my dear friend Donna, and everything changed from that point.

I decided that I wasn't going to 'settle' and be defeated by a minor inconvenience. I needed to go deep within me, to find the lion - to change my entire life.

Keep Going Always™ was born...

I did acknowledge how I felt and what was going on. I dealt with it all day by day, by taking each 5mins as it was and doing the best I could. I started to recite affirmations to myself and boost and motivate myself into a positive mindset and continued, with guidance from my other dear friend Andrea, to really show up for my son, be his voice and learn more to help Dominic's life living in this society and world.

I got Dominic in a placement within a special school in Merseyside. Dominic was also a page boy at my wedding (he coped as well as he could), and then we moved down south to Wiltshire in the UK where Dominic attended specialist schools and a specialist college (over the years), all with me by his side, kicking ass with the system that's in place, and working very closely with some amazing teachers, as I truly believe home and school go hand in hand. Whatever goes on at home affects school, and vice versa. So, working with the school helps tremendously.

And now, as I write this chapter, my son is 23 years old, and I haven't stopped since. I am his full-time carer, and I have helped numerous families over the years to be a voice for their own children. The one piece of advice I'd give you, if you are in this position is to "Follow your gut and don't take no for an answer".

So, Keep Going Always™ was born in 1999, powered up even more in 2000 and 2001 with the autism journey (which I'm still on now), but I've always had Keep Going Always™ within me from when I was a child. I am from a generation of powerful women, all the way up my family tree blood line and I am so proud.

My beautiful Mum inspired me that, even as a single parent, you can achieve anything. She taught me to never give up on your goals and she was an incredible nurse and mentor to many during her career. Mum also taught me to go after all my desires and dreams and to keep pushing through with determination, especially when I joined the British Army and then with my own business. She always believed in me, of which I am truly grateful.

My Mum walked me down the aisle, danced with me down Broadway in NYC to Frank Sinatra's "New York, New York" song, showed me that you can overcome anything, and everything thrown your way and that you can solo-travel the world and make memories. My Mum was an unstoppable Warrior Queen, always smiling, right to the end and I am so blessed to have her as my Mum.

My incredible Nan showed me that you can be a strong, independent woman regardless of your circumstances and just because we didn't have much growing up, we were still worthy of respect. Nan was strict but fair and you didn't want her to stare at you a certain way otherwise you knew you'd be in trouble. You didn't backchat or be rude and you addressed people with their title, correctly. You dressed smart, said your manners, and sat up straight, with elbows off the table when you were eating. I am privileged to have had a Nan like that.

You see, at one point within my life my Mum and I were homeless, and I was carrying my teddy and stool, my Mum had her handbag and a carrier bag full of our clothes as we climbed the road to where my Nan lived, and Mum knocked on the door. My Nan took us in, and we were taken care of despite everything going on.

My Mum and Nan were incredible role models for me, and I will be forever grateful to them for cementing within the core of me that no matter what goes on in your life – you are strong and can come through the other side of anything. They were "grafters", and so am I. You pull up your sleeves and get the job completed yourself.

Keep Going Always™ has always helped me throughout the years, amid all my trials and tribulations and it's the driving force, source, and the core within me.

The one thing that I'd like to share with you is that strength, power, focus and determination can be instilled in you when you decide to say YES to yourself and start your journey into high level mindset work. Anything and everything can be accomplished within all arenas of your life through MINDSET.

No matter what the circumstances are. No matter what others think or say. No matter your past and what you've been through. Set an intention that, right here, right now, in this present moment, that you can and will do anything you set your mind to – whatever you desire and deserve in your future is yours.

You are here to live a truly phenomenal, abundant, and great life filled with happiness, kindness, love, and joy, and not forgetting respect and appreciation too. Good health, wealth, and money and all the goodness can be yours when you move forward with certainty and conviction.

You can do it! Be mindful and respectful and know you can have the best life possible when you make the decision. Don't sway or let any doubts creep into your head. For inspiration please watch the "Keep Going Always" Video here - https://www.youtube.com/watch?v=ugdKwNIruz8

Do NOT allow a "STOP SIGN" to hold YOU back in YOUR life from achieving anything YOU want.

SMASH THROUGH THE STOP SIGN OF YOUR LIFE. I will be cheering you on.

DEDICATION

To my son Dominic, for all that you are, I deeply love you. Thank you for choosing me to be your Mum and I vow to protect you and be your voice until my last breath. xx

Rebecca Adams

Rebecca Adams wears her heart on her sleeve, is real and raw, and always flows in alignment through her life and business. She kicks ass at what she does, and she is focused on empowering as many people as possible, to feel alive and live a phenomenal life through gaining control of their mindset so that they can align deeply with their true soul work, be themselves and earn money whilst doing it.

Her mission is to give more people the mindset, skillset, and tools to gain more clarity, focus and confidence to master their life in all arenas, through flow, ease and enjoyment to align more with their soul and doing the inner work needed.

Rebecca has been in business for over 18 years, and she is all about empowering, inspiring and motivating people to say YES to themselves and live in a high energy mindset in flow and ease, to create more abundance, to be a voice and to trust the process. She lives and breathes the Law of Attraction daily and is focused on giving as much value as possible to her audience, in all arenas and on all her platforms.

She is the International Life, Business & Mindset Mastery Mentor™ for people who want to create personal and financial freedom. She is a Law of Attraction Practitioner, NLP Practitioner, Belief Clearing Practitioner, Author, Speaker, Motivator and Businesswoman. She builds websites, creates online programs & helps people monetize their ideas.

Rebecca changes people's lives through her Transformational Digital Online Programs, High-end Private Bespoke Coaching & Mentoring. She also has an online membership club called Ignite Academy which is jampacked full of amazing transformational content.

She is the Creative Director & Founder of the Empowerment Convention IGNITE Live Event which is a life-changing event with speakers, a gala dinner and entertainment, held in the Roman City of Bath, UK.

Rebecca is an award winning entrepreneur, #1 International best-selling co-author, and masters in mindset. Unlike other personal development experts, she focuses on aligning every area of your life so that you can confidently transform your life, be at peace and have everything you desire.

She is a Mum to 2 amazing incredible human beings, a Special Needs Mum, a UK Army Veteran and she lives in the UK. She loves to travel, read, listen to music, take photographs, watch movies and make endless memories. She was a dedicated daughter to her inspirational Mum Carole who passed away in April 2021.

Rebecca was nominated for the 2019 Boots Wellness Warrior of the Year Award and the 2019 Businesswoman of the Year Award. She was also nominated for 2 awards in the Digital Women Awards 2021.

WEB LINKS:

Website: https://www.rebeccaadamsbiz.com
Business Facebook Page: https://www.facebook.com/rebeccaadams187
Personal Facebook Wall: https://www.facebook.com/rebecca.adams.39108/
Online Digital Course Website: http://racourses.thinkific.com/
Linktree: https://linktr.ee/rebeccaadams187
Instagram: https://www.instagram.com/rebeccaadams187
Pinterest: https://www.pinterest.com/rebeccaadams187
Clubhouse: @rebeccaadams187

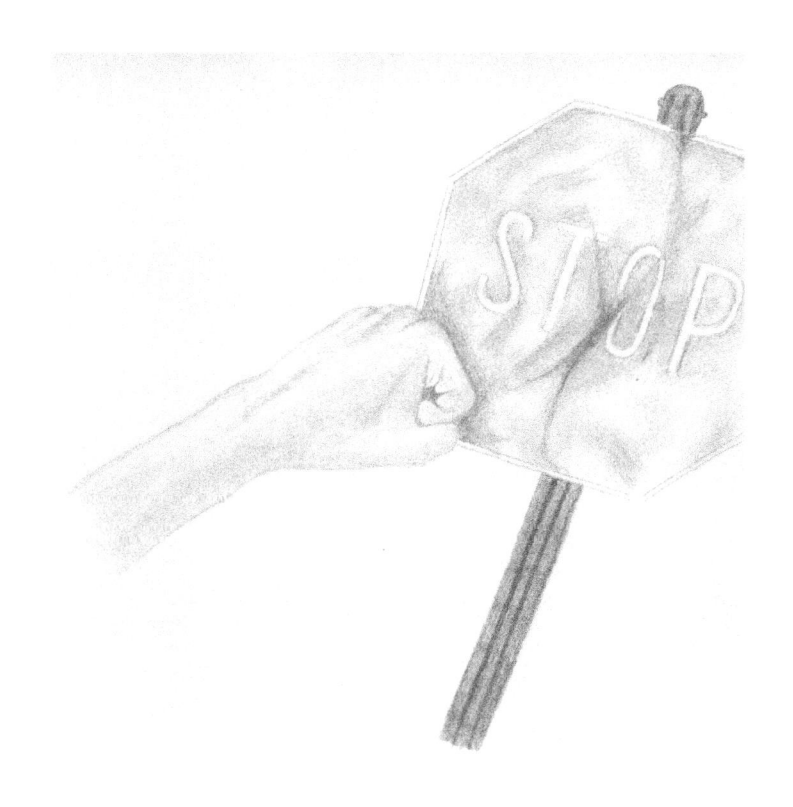

"My reality now is what I make it, what I design & my conscious state is awake & thriving"

Phoebe Adams

Conscious State: Switching Reality

During the pandemic my mum had told me that we were moving away, like miles away. I remember I couldn't handle the decision she had made and attempted to get out of it.

I looked at places I could live on my own, live with a friend, get a job - it just wasn't going to work.

The life I enjoyed in my town and county was great but temporary. Of course, in that moment I didn't know that my world was crumbling down, and I was slipping away from everything I knew, and it went very quickly.

I am grateful to my mum as she allowed me to go out and enjoy the remainder of my time, whilst she was packing up the house, as she knew how hard it was for me to leave, due to it being the only place I'd known and lived. I knew the people, the people knew me, the status, the groups of mates, the drama, my memories - the good and bad ones. It was leaving me, or I was leaving it.

I remember my final day there. It was emotional but I never let that get to me.

I had the house to myself, as my Mum had travelled up north to take my brother to stay with my Grandma and Grandad. My mum allowed me to have a friend or two over to stay, for comfort, as long as we kept it clean. That night I could leave reality one more time, have the moment with my mates, calling others, playing the Wii, watching the sunset through my large living room window with a recognisable view, for one last time.

That night was the moment I knew no one could know. I didn't want people knowing I left. I told very few friends, to refrain from drama, reminding me that I left my life behind. Once my mates had left, I walked around my house once more to remember all the times we have had in the house and if you thought I was emotional then, the drive up north with my mum was a nightmare.

My mum had packed a few last bits from the house into the back of the car. I said goodbye to the best neighbour in the world who lived across the road, and we started to drive away. I was crying silently in the car looking around at my home, at everything I knew. It was a huge punch in the gut that I was leaving. My tears had paused through the 3-hour long journey, before beginning again when seeing the new hometown. My thought process wasn't much. I instantly thought the place would look better underwater as all I could see was old people and mouldy corner shops.

The first month living there was horrendous. I was a typical stroppy teenager just with a valid reason to be like that. My family were making small attempts to get me liking the place and I really did appreciate it. Taking me around town, to places where they used to live, some shops and nice places to walk. My head and heart were having a stubborn argument with each other to accept this is the new home or to keep rejecting it. My mum allowed me to take trips back down south to my old town to see my friends and stay with them for a while, it was so refreshing. I saw so many people and made so many memories…

I relied on friends a lot. I tend to make friends my soul purpose. I'm the type of person who will do anything just to have a good time with my friends and create memories with no regrets. It doesn't matter if we are just chilling in bed doing nothing, as long as we have good vibes, I'm happy. I was too happy I was blind.

Once I returned to my new home, it all went dark. My heart sunk into my stomach, the headphones went in my ears and the Lucozade addiction began. The more I went down south, the more I was attached that when I came back home, I wasn't me. I wasn't eating healthy or working out. I sat on my butt all day, I wasn't great and was physically alone. At this point in time I was stuck, battling myself between accepting the new or keeping hold of the old. It was pizza or burgers, red or blue pill, Mercedes, or BMW, it didn't come to me until…

My Grandma got sick. She started to seriously get ill and even more of my life was slipping away. My Grandma was the whole reason we moved; my Grandma IS the whole reason we are here.

She was the funniest little woman ever. The smartest no doubt.

Whenever I had a question to do with science, maths, geography, or health she was the woman to go to. I loved it when she would smack people with facts, like watching a gameshow like "The Chase", and my Grandma would rinse into anyone who didn't know answers she classed as obvious. Always cracking some joke at me being silly or dumb but she knew I was really intelligent, (well, I pick and choose my moments), but she still knew I was a smart kid.

My Grandma would always be the life of the party and she enjoyed cooking and doing things for everyone. Although we would tell her to relax, she would hit us with a witty line and go do it herself. My Grandma liked helping and feeling needed, right until the end. I like that my Grandma was supportive of me being vegan and healthy and so I knew that I had to step back into my ways. Healthier ways.

I dropped my Lucozade addiction, started getting up early, working out and pushing myself, eating healthy and stuck to a routine. I got creative and started doing more drawings - my Grandma loved my drawings. I even decided to try and get out to make friends. I was going to town and walking around, learning the route on my own, getting ready to build the courage and talk to people that looked my age. My plan didn't work but it was definitely worth a try!

I still wasn't okay. My head wasn't okay, my friends down south were dropping one by one, and I had no one to talk to. Mum was always working in her office and my brother kept himself private anyways. There was no point in social media and not only was I now physically alone, but mentally alone too. I was hurting inside but refused to let it show. I still worked out but was not motivated. I still ate right but had no satisfaction. I was still trying to see the light at the end of a tunnel that seemed like it was the channel to France.

My Grandma was getting worse, which meant my mum was getting stressed trying to do all the things and it was a lot for my brother to take in. My grandad was worrying, and I felt like it was all crumbling beneath my feet, and I'm not trained to play 'the floor is lava' unlike some. I couldn't figure it out - what I needed - I didn't know if I even needed someone, something or if I needed to be somewhere.

My thought process was trying to become stronger on my own, but that's it, that's what I was doing. I was building my discipline by making me stick to my healthy food plan and workouts, but I still wasn't fulfilled. I thought this was it, the rest of my life living here, alone and on my own, not moving anywhere in life.

One day in December I took a stab in the dark at this "teenager tinder" type thing but I was looking for some friends. I created an account and got in contact with a few people from the north and had a laugh on a few people's live videos they put on there. But someone came into the live video from the town I live in! I instantly jumped on the case, and we got on really well! To keep it safe we exchanged numbers and got on FaceTime (to ensure neither of us were some old creep on an app for teens). We arranged to meet up and she brought some of her friends and that night was added to my list of "Important Days to Remember For Life"

That day I met that thing I needed. That one thing I was missing in my life to open my eyes to my reality. I couldn't have been more grateful for my new conscious state. I had woken up to the new, the fresh and the best thing for me.

Over time we got closer and closer. We clicked. The spark was there, and my reality was beaming. It was enhanced. I had realised that I deserve this person - my person. I earned him, from having a drive for my future and still not giving up, a healthy lifestyle and dedicating my day to exercise, disciplining myself, the emotions I had been through, the abandonment that happened to me and I get him. I deserve him.

And it's been many months since we first met. I still only have him, but that's all I need. Because I was willing to let go of my old life and open a new one (for me who is quite stubborn, that can be a challenge), but I couldn't be more grateful. He taught me that I am the only one I need and that if it cannot be fixed there and then, to not stress. If it is not my problem, then don't even think about it. It's okay to be sad unless it's a happy moment and to take any opportunity - even if you're scared. The list goes on and on, and the lessons and blessings keep rolling in. My reality now is what I make it, what I design, and my conscious state is awake and thriving.

It is unreal how we all react when something suddenly happens and can flip our lives a full 360 degrees.

Our instant reaction is to revert back to where we are happy and comfortable. We want to sit in our safe zone and still ask for change. When change happens, it is unpredictable as we think it's the end of the world and want the old way back.

I don't know what it is but the word new isn't nice unless it's clothes, food, or gadgets. I encourage anyone who is wanting change to expect heartbreak, failure, success, laughter, tears, relief, stress, and any other mess you can imagine.

Change will come in with a big boulder and crush an entire city.
But will that city be destroyed forever? No.
Will it be rebuilt better? Potentially.
Is the choice up to you? Absolutely.

DEDICATION

To you, the reader. Don't think too much about change - just embrace it. Sit down, enjoy the journey, and focus on you because you could be rewarded, and you won't even realise it.

Phoebe Adams

Phoebe Adams is a model, blogger, artist and book cover illustrator and young entrepreneur in the UK. She's very big on taking care of your skin – no matter your age. She also loves to travel, go to the gym, cook delicious meals, and enjoy life.

In her blog she loves to write about skincare, food and nutrition, exercise, and lifestyle. She is vegan and loves to share her passion for veganism.

Phoebe has drawn the illustration to the front covers of the published books "Smashing Through the Glass Ceiling", "Smashing Through the Brick Wall" and also this book, "Smashing Through the Stop Sign of Life".

WEBLINKS:

Website – www.phoebeadamsbiz.com
Instagram – www.instagram.com/phoebeadams_
TikTok - adamsphoebe

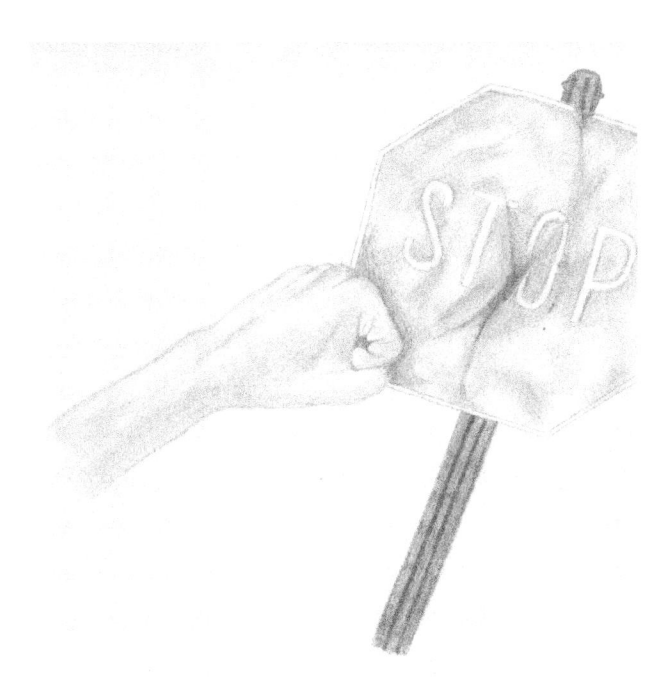

"Always remember no matter what, you are stronger than you think you are! You have overcome every hurdle you have faced"

Maria Harris

A routine visit to the Dr's changed everything

Let's start with taking you back to March 2019, when life became oh so very different in a matter of hours.

You know the kind of different where you need to pinch yourself to make sure you're still in the real world and not dreaming?!

What I am about to tell you is by far the worst thing I have ever had to deal with! That is including losing both my parents and going through the bereavement process of that whilst being an only sibling, and in 2015, an orphan.

So, to set you up for this chapter imagine this for a moment…
An only child and single mother, with no family support, completely on my own

(besides a few very close friends), and working in a job for the NHS, where you are trained to pick up on Safeguarding issues.

After a routine visit to the Doctors in December 2018, the doctor originally diagnosed RL with skin tags in the first appointment and advised if they did not disappear or if they got worse, to go back to the doctors.

So, after monitoring these skin tags over a period of 3 months, they indeed got bigger, and a lot more appeared as well…… Following the original advice from the Doctor, I made an appointment to take my daughter back to have these skin tags re-assessed. What I was not prepared for, or even expected to happen next, became a whole new outlook on my life!!

It was in early March 2019, on a second appointment with the nurse when I was asked if it was okay for the Doctor to come take a look. Of course, I agreed and thought she is just getting a second opinion or asking what medication can be prescribed for a 2-year-old child.

The Doctor came in and then asked me to go to her room where she would go through a few things with me and if my friend could take RL back to the car. At this point I was thinking to myself; "What on earth is going on?", "Why do I need to go into a different room and let my best friend take my daughter back to the car?".

I was about to learn why….

The Doctor then started to ask me lots of questions regarding a significant person in RL's life and whether anything had happened to her? Was there any sexual abuse?

As you can imagine at this point, my head was doing somersaults, my tummy churning, shaking, and thinking what the hell was wrong with her.
The Doctor then advised me that she believed there was a high possibility it was

Genital Warts. Shocked, speechless, and not knowing what on earth to think, the doctor advised me that an urgent appointment needed to be made with the paediatrician at the local hospital and SS (Social Services) had to be called in, as Genital Warts are only contracted through sexual contact or sexual abuse.

After hearing this I completely broke down. My broken heart was sobbing, and I started blaming myself, together with questioning everything and everyone – especially myself. "Who on earth has touched RL?" "Where have I gone wrong?", "Should I have gone back to work when she was 10 months old?", "Should I have let her out my sight and let her stay overnight with certain people?". The list of initial thoughts and questions was endless and far too many to be named.

After composing myself, I came out of the Doctors surgery and got into my car. I looked at my innocent 2-year-old and cried. My best friend asked me what on earth was wrong and I could not speak. No words would come out of my mouth to explain. I could not tell her what was going on at that point. I could just about manage to say, "I'll tell you when we get home".

When we got home, (it was only around the corner), I got RL out the car and cuddled her so tightly and just began crying, my heart breaking once more. "How on earth was I going to explain to my best friend and my work what the hell was going on?!" After all, I was trained in Safeguarding issues for adults and children. Initial thoughts ringing in my head of; "I clearly can't keep my daughter safe, how the hell can I do my job?".

My best friend looked at me and said, "Mate what's going on? what's wrong?". Sobbing and still cuddling my daughter I answered, "They believe she's got genital warts and think she could have been sexually abused!!" My best mate's face was a picture of shock and she started to cry. All 3 of us ended up having a group cuddle, as I was not putting RL down at that moment.

It then sunk in, and I thought to myself, "Wait, I have not done anything wrong. Let me ring SS (Social Services) and get ahead of them and get this sorted out".

So, that's exactly what I did. I rang SS and spoke to their emergency team who started to do some digging, found the report, and commented on how quickly I reacted to the situation and for getting in touch with them before they had even looked at the report to action anything. SS then went through an initial assessment with me on the phone and advised me to not let her out of my sight or leave her with anyone until further notice.

I then rang my work. Thankfully it was my actual manager who was in work that day and I explained everything to him and advised I wouldn't be in for at least the next 2 or 3 weeks. I would arrange a sicknote to cover me, but I had to deal with what I have been told and I had to protect RL.

That whole evening had me wondering who I could trust? Can I trust my best friend? Can I trust my small support bubble? Who, just who, could I trust? Was my whole life as a mother a lie? Were my friends, my friends?

This thought process went on for hours, days and even weeks from the start of this process and at times still has me questioning people. I never had much trust or patience with new people anyway before this situation, but now this made this thought process even worse.

Within a few days, after the visit from SS, everyone who had been around RL were to be investigated. My best friend who lived with me had completed a risk assessment previously, so they didn't need to check as much with her, but as she had RL the most, due to me working, she was the top person to be investigated. She was quickly ruled out and I was again allowed to leave her with RL. This process took a week itself but felt like a lifetime.

The whole week period with having this all going on, my best friend was getting worried and upset, as she knew she had not done anything wrong, and it became an incredibly stressful and anxious time for all of us.

Now, if you're a parent you'll know that it wasn't going to be easy to let RL out of my sight for even 5 minutes let alone a trip to the shop. My best friend was ruled to be the only person to be left with RL besides myself for around 5 months.

I had a call from SS (Social Services) around 11am one day, to say they had managed to get an appointment at the local hospital at 2.30pm that afternoon and to attend and meet my Social Worker there. Until this point nothing was proven that it was genital warts, so it was all still based on the process it was.

The drive to the local hospital would take roughly 30 minutes depending on traffic. That 30-minute drive took forever. The car was in silence all the way. The thoughts that were going round in my head at that time are indescribable, but if I had to explain, I'd say think about what you'd be thinking in this situation, and you would probably be somewhere near. Arriving at the hospital and parking the car, my heart pounding and my body shaking coming back on, I knew this was going to be one of the hardest parts of this process.

Upon entering the hospital and heading to the ward, my heart sinking even more each step I took, deep breathing to calm me down, we arrived at our destination. We were sent to the opposite side of the waiting area where RL could play with some toys. Sat there waiting to see my Social Worker and the Doctor.

This wait was like going to hell and back again. I actually felt sick to my stomach.

Upon seeing my Social Worker's face, she came across and explained the process and that RL would be examined, and it was only to be me and RL allowed in the room.

Walking into the room, I was greeted by 2 Doctors and my Social Worker. They went through a lot of questions - some general and some abrasive questions too. My Social Worker was writing everything down and asking questions as well as myself, as we both knew I was not going to take everything in. Next was the bit I was dreading - The Examination.

I will not go into details as that part will never leave my head, but RL was then diagnosed in late March 2019 with Genital Warts around her anus, which was diagnosed on that day.

The paediatrician advised that although nothing could be proved, as there are no tests to prove yes or no, there was a very high chance it was by someone close to her, especially if they had previous. However, everyone in my support bubble that had been around RL were still under investigation besides my best friend who had already been ruled as all clear. Social Services were aware of situations regarding a couple of people who had been around my daughter, so advised me of this and they were not allowed to be left unattended, at any point with her, even now - 2 years on.

As you can imagine the thought process, I had to go through was horrendous! "Why RL? What has she done so wrong? She is only an innocent baby. Who can I trust? Who has betrayed me? Who can I talk to? Where can I go? Who is safe to be with my daughter?"

I was advised that the Genital Warts can reappear at any point throughout RL's life. If they do reappear, I was advised they would probably disappear on their own, which is what happened about a year later, with no medical intervention needed.

Amongst all the other information I was given that day, I also was advised that RL would never be able to give birth naturally as she can pass the warts down to her children. My thought process soon became extremely hard, very quickly. Imagine being told this information and having to try and process this with everything else going on as well!

Straight away my thoughts turned to her, "Oh my god what have I let happen? She can now never experience natural childbirth, because of me I've taken that away from her!" Of course, I knew that it is not my fault, and it is not me who has taken that right away from her. It is whoever has done this to my child.

After several visits and appointments with Social Services, it was agreed that the only person besides myself that could have RL who was involved with her, was my best friend. Of course, there are a couple of friends who did not need to be investigated as they'd never had her on their own.

The case with Social Services was eventually closed in November 2019 after lots of meetings, progress reports, courses, circles of safety and even now I will never ever know what's happened to RL. Social Services have a belief of who they feel it is, that may have done something to RL. However, it cannot and will never ever be proven so no one could be prosecuted or arrested for it! Again, this is a game-changer on knowing that nothing can be done to gain closure and find out exactly what happened to my gorgeous 2-year-old.

Although the relief of Social Services closing the case and knowing it wasn't my fault and to not feel guilty about it is a relief, I will never, ever, gain closure for my own thoughts and will always have the question in my head, "Was it you?" when I am around certain people.

Whilst this process was going on, I reached out to try and find groups or networks to help people in this situation on how to handle and deal with the pain, emotions and trust issues caused by this. And do you know what? There isn't anything out there besides therapy groups, which aren't necessarily aimed for this kind of trauma. So, although they provide a talking aspect to it, they don't cover the aspects of what to expect in later life with your child as they grow up and develop their own friendships, relationships, and work commitments.

During this whole process I had NO-ONE I could turn to for help or advice or support, as no-one I knew had experienced this before, so I only had me. For anyone with a partner or family network it is a hard process but trying to process this by yourself is even harder.

My quote has always been "Always remember no matter what, you are stronger than you think you are!". But since the situation of 2019, I have added a bit onto my quote. So, my full quote I now live by and keep reminding myself of is: "Always remember no matter what, you are stronger than you think you are! YOU have overcome every hurdle you have faced."

So, let's bring you back to 2020 - the year everyone will remember. I made the choice to protect RL fully and not allow this incident to hinder and hold me or her back, for the rest of our lives and live in worry every time the back gate opened or someone knocked on the front door.

I packed myself, my daughter, and my best friend up and moved out of Wiltshire and made the move to a different country and restart life in Swansea. Moving 3 days before Christmas according to everyone was crazy and I was mad for even doing it, but do you know what? They aren't me. They don't know what demons kept creeping up every time something triggered it all. I wanted that fresh start and most importantly WE needed it.

Ever since this situation I've been worried about going back to work as employers generally would never understand that there would be times I needed to be with my daughter and have her close. So, I took my adventure one step further and launched my business in April 2021 to work from home, so I am always near to my daughter and can keep an eye on her and if she struggles with school because of this, I can be there within minutes to calm her and do what's needed, to let her still be a child.

I honestly hope no-one ever has to go through this situation themselves, but always remember that someone will be there for you so please don't suffer in silence. Mental Health is dangerous and holding things in can make it worse so always remember #SpeakoutReachout.

DEDICATION

I dedicate this chapter and everything I do to my absolutely amazing, beautiful daughter RL. Always remember baby girl, Mummy's Got your Back always and that's never changing. Love you always princess.
Love Mummy xxxx

Maria Harris

Maria is a single mum to daughter RL. She lives in Swansea in Wales, although she grew up in Wiltshire. She enjoys listening to music and watching films in her spare time. She also enjoys spending quality time with her daughter and friends.

In 2021 she embarked on a new journey in Wales and starting her own business to work from home. She started Little Ruby's Treats, which is a Printing Service and IT Expertise Business. The Business offers a Printing Service, Sweet Treats and now the added section to include her IT Help and Advice section, which breaks down into IT Coaching, Website Builds and Logo Creations.

The business is growing, and Maria is really excited about helping more clients worldwide with her products and services. She is also a No1 International Best-Selling Author with her first chapter in "Smashing Through the Brick Wall" and a Blogger.
WEBLINKS:

Website: www.littlerubystreats.co.uk

Personal Facebook: https://www.facebook.com/Shortie69/

Business Facebook: https://www.facebook.com/groups/lrtreats

Instagram: https://www.instagram.com/treatslittlerubys/

Linktree: https://linktr.ee/Littlerubystreats

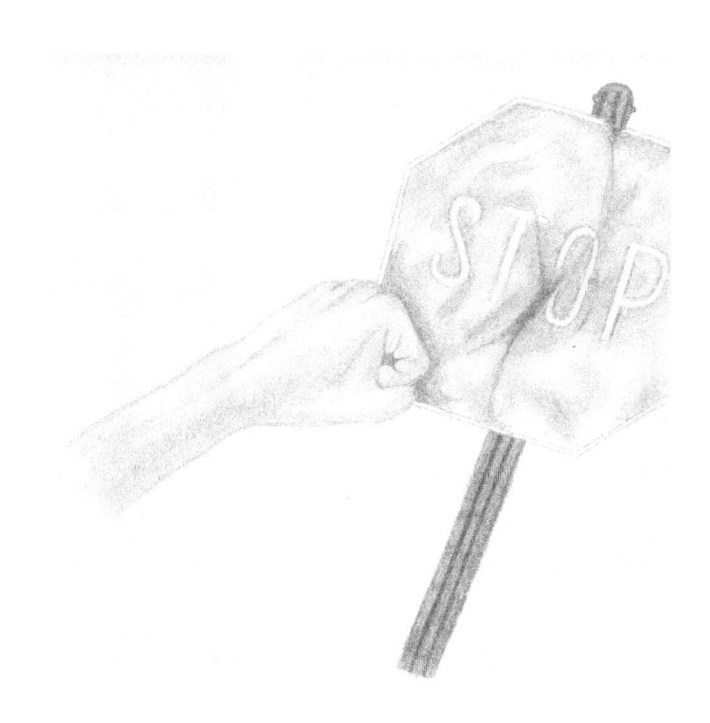

" When you take back control of your own destiny you create your own magic"

Ray Coates & Michelle Roche

They May Have Pulled the Plug, but they'll NEVER switch us off

<u>Ray</u>

It wasn't the first time that I stood at the kitchen window. In fact, over the last few months and year, I had improved the ability to stand at a kitchen window, in a grateful and mindful way.

Michelle, Shady the dog and I had been living on a caravan park for over a year. It wasn't exactly where we wished to live; in fact, in the weeks leading up to this mindful window moment, I'd developed a feeling and sense of being uncomfortable in the caravan. However, I plunged my hands into the sink and reminded myself of the gratitude I needed to feel for the shelter we were currently living in.

Whilst I had begun to feel uncomfortable in our home, nothing had prepared me for the massive upheaval that would unfold.

It was looking like it was going to be an extremely hot day. Michelle had gone to work. She'd started a job in a local care home at the beginning of the year. As I washed the morning cups in the bowl, I noticed a couple of police officers walk past the window. Very soon a couple of police officers had grown into well over double figures (more than likely 20) and they were surrounding a collection of men and women, smartly dressed, and carrying clipboards.

We lived in a gated community, which had not been without trouble on several of the adjacent plots, but overall was a safe place to live. I didn't have to be a detective to realise, something was going down. Brushing this off as none of my business, I finished the washing up and went to put the kettle on to make a drink. 'Strange. No electricity. Oh well must be a power cut', I thought.

It became ever apparent that this "official army", were making their way around the various site plots and knocking on every door.

The next few hours were a literal blur, after they had knocked on the door and broke the unbelievable news to me! How was I going to tell Michelle? After all, she'd only just gone to work on a 'normal day' and I already knew, nothing was going to be 'normal' for a while, after this news.

Michelle

I finished my shift at 2pm and couldn't wait to get in the car and put on the air conditioning. The temperature was in the 30's and I'd spent the last hour of my shift helping out in the kitchen. Washing up time was my least favourite part of the day!
I couldn't wait to get back home; Ray would have an ice-cold drink ready for me when I walked in.

As I drove in through the open gates, I followed the road round to our plot. I was completely unaware of the morning's events. Parking the car outside our plot, I grabbed my bags and walked through the open gates and into our caravan. What came next took me by complete surprise; Ray said, 'I think you need to sit down'.

I could tell by the look on his face, that what he was about to tell me, was not good news. He started off by telling me that we had no power and that the electricity supply had been switched off. Ray had been at home with Shady when the authorities arrived, there were lots of Police, council officials, the RSPCA and of course the electricity company.

He'd been given a number to contact the housing for assistance. We had no other information, and our landlord was not answering his phone. Our neighbours didn't know anymore either and we were all just waiting for some news.

Ray

Over the next few days, I went into organisation mode. Responsibility fell on me to proceed with arrangements as Michelle was working. In these days I felt angry at our circumstances. This was not our fault. However, I also had an inner energy drawing me to realise we must continue in gratitude and work with these enforced changes.
We needed to make arrangements for Shady, as one of the first offers we were given was a Travelodge hotel and they wouldn't accept dogs. The caravan was so hot and as Michelle continued to work, I felt like I was being forced to make a decision with our future housing.

It came to light that one of our neighbours (he had one of the only caravans fitted with gas), had been told 2 days prior to the police, council, and power companies' arrival, that they couldn't deliver any gas to him. Clearly this was a planned eviction operation, and we were in the middle of it. My mind raced between pragmatic practical thoughts and the unbelievably emotional wrenching of extreme uncertainty.

One conversation with the council that deeply affected me, was regarding my sons' visitation. As I looked to potentially accept and organise council accommodation, I explained that every other weekend, for over a decade, I'd had legal access and visitation with my sons.

The explanation I received from an individual at the council knocked me off my feet.
'By law we don't have to accommodate your sons, as they already have a home'. Emotionally winded, I knew we would need to take action. A 'leap

of faith' would be required. Private rental was not an option in the South of England, due to prices and I'd had to cease my self-employed job as a driving instructor, due to 'lockdown' restrictions. Additionally, I was setting off in my creative purpose and beginning to set up elements of a business through mine and Michelle's creativity.

In all of this, I felt alone in not being able to provide a home for my sons, Michelle and Shady. I wrestled with decisions of where do I go? and even where do I belong? Strength was needed, not doubt. Faith was needed not fear. Nevertheless, being human and having experienced homelessness before, this was an unbelievable challenge to every part of my soul and fibre.

Michelle

It was so hot in the caravan. Everything was electric and with no power, we had no fans and no fridge. The food in the freezer had already started to defrost and the heat was unbearable. Our neighbours were just as bewildered. A storm was brewing and a few of us sat together outside in the cooling rain. The realisation dawned on us that tonight we would have no power, but we bonded as a community, sharing candles, food, and drinks. The atmosphere was upbeat and there was a real sense of community spirit and togetherness. Many of our neighbours were Romanian and although we exchanged pleasantries, we never really got to know them until now.
Going to bed that night we were filled with the hope that by the morning, the power would be back on.

I was up at 6am to get ready for my shift - still no power. This meant I wouldn't be able to have my usual mug of coffee; there would be no toast for breakfast and no hot water for a shower. Stepping into the cold shower definitely took the place of coffee in waking me up, not an option I would choose again though. It had been a hot sticky night, with no fans to keep the caravan cool. Poor Shady was clearly struggling, with not just the heat, she knew something wasn't right.

Another hot day in work over, Ray came to pick me up. It made sense that he had the car so he could charge his phone and cool off with the air con. How was I going to wash my uniform? I couldn't wash it in cold water, as we'd had instruction from work that uniforms had to be put on a hot wash! I had one last clean uniform; hopefully the power would be back on tomorrow. We were in the midst of the first 'lockdown', which limited our choices for supplies and also meant the launderette was not open.

The landlord had been and explained the situation; it became clear that we were not going to be getting power back any time soon. It seems someone living on a different plot had been stealing electricity. Our plot was all legal and above board, yet we were being punished too. We had a decision to make, Ray made phone calls whilst I was at work.

Once again, I'd gone to work on an empty stomach; thankfully, by arriving early, I was able to make myself a coffee at work. Ray was going to find a storage unit and spend the day packing and moving our belongings. This was the first step to gaining some control of our lives. I saw the car pull into the carpark and couldn't wait to get out of work and find out if there was any news. Ray had just come back from the storage unit but there were many more trips needed.

We made a decision; we could no longer stay where we were. Ray had called the number he'd been given and started the process. One thing he had been told was that we would not be offered accommodation that allowed dogs. I called my daughters and arranged for them to take care of Shady. This meant that after the hectic day we'd both had, we had to drive to a location close to Birmingham, which was a halfway point. In the darkness of a lay-by, I handed Shady over to them. I had no idea when or if I would see my old girl again. At fourteen years old she was doing well, but she was struggling. It was a very difficult time, I felt like I was just abandoning my most faithful and loyal friend. I was feeling angry that we had been forced into this position through no fault of our own.

Another shift over and another one began. There was more packing and more trips to the storage unit to be done. We couldn't leave our belongings unattended for long, as our plot was no longer secure. The Police had cut through the lock and chain when they gained entry. On our return from the storage unit Ray received a phone call, we had been offered a flat in Milton Keynes. Ray dropped me back at the caravan and went to collect the keys for the flat. I continued to pack our belongings into black bin bags, whilst trying to think what we would need to take with us. It's not as easy as it sounds when you don't know where you're going to be placed. We were aware that we could be moved on from the flat at any moment.

I was feeling a little anxious and couldn't wait for Ray to arrive back. The landlord was outside, and he was unaware that we were leaving. He had asked us to "stick it out". Easier said than done but after all, this was his business - his livelihood. He was a lovely guy and I really felt for him and the situation he now faced but this battle was not ours to fight. We broke the news to him together as soon as Ray got back, and he gave us a hug and wished us the best in our future.

Ray

I arrived back with the keys. Michelle and I filled the car and made the first 2-hour round trip. When you experience poor living conditions, it's not a great feeling. In our situation, I was visited by the presence of guilt again. It was bad enough me experiencing these temporary emergency housing conditions, but no way did I desire for Michelle and my sons to have to live in this place. I explained as best I could to Michelle what the place was like. And, whilst I took no blame for our situation, I felt a very heightened level of responsibility to prepare Michelle for what she was going to face.

The flat was on the second floor and there was no lift. The smell in the stairwell was awful, to say the least. We later discovered it was coming from the bin shed. It was one of those smells that sticks inside you for ages. I did the best I could to help Michelle with the challenge of getting our things inside as she was on her feet all day and her job in care was taking its toll on her joints. The front door had been repaired but it was obvious that it had been kicked in (the bathroom door had also been kicked in). Clearly this place had bad history and we could feel it. This added to my feeling of being less. How could Michelle and my boys be subjected to living in a potentially unsafe environment like this?

Talk about out of the frying pan and into the fire. We were trying to survive and in fact not just survive but thrive, in ever darkening circumstances. Yet, we still maintained gratitude, love, and a powerful sense of destiny, in these fragile, uncertain, and vulnerable moments.

We had to take several trips up and down the stairs. This became, for me, a lion's share type pilgrimage, as I felt the need to take the physical burden of what was not my fault. Throughout this all there was never any blame from Michelle - quite the opposite.

I knew we had to make massive decisions and Michelle's work was not viable for so many reasons. Yet, my work had changed, and I needed to continue with my purpose, my calling - we both did. We both knew this wasn't a permanent place and we could've been moved at any time. We were homeless; we were officially counted as homeless! My goodness me, the plug had been pulled, yet we still created and aimed for our destiny purpose.

Michelle

I looked into bus routes but as we were in 'lockdown', not all buses were running. Milton Keynes was a long way from work. So, it was decided that I definitely needed to use the car. I spoke with my manager to see if I could take some time off work and thankfully, he was both sympathetic and supportive. I took a week off on annual leave, which gave me some time to take in our situation. Here we were in a strange area, feeling angry about our experience, there was very little information from anyone. I was told that this was the closest place they could offer to where I was working. "Where I was working" I said out loud, as I recalled how the nation was encouraged to clap for the NHS, care workers and all the other key workers. Several of our neighbours were key workers, including me, yet here we were being made homeless and treated like we were the virus. I couldn't allow these feelings to stay, I had to acknowledge them and let them go. A positive mindset was needed in order for us to get through this extremely difficult situation.

Did we allow any of this to stop us from creating? No, we certainly did not.

Ray and I released our e-book of poetry, our G.L.A.D journal. Throughout all the stress of what we'd been going through, we continued our creative journey together. We filmed a video in the flat, which was posted on social media, where we talked about our e-book release. I even created the front and back cover for the amazing author Jenny Ford's 'Write to Release Journal'. All of my art supplies were somewhere in storage, so I went shopping and bought some more. No one really knew the whole truth of what we were experiencing. We were so grateful for all we had including our special guest, the rat in the kitchen!! I'm not talking about the UB40 song; thankfully he only visited us once, we think.

The day had come where I worked my last ever shift and Ray was outside, with the car full of the belongings we thought we would need to take with us. We had to leave everything else in the storage unit. My tears were flowing as I said my final goodbye to the colleagues who had become my friends, especially my dear friend Trina. Working throughout 'lockdown' had brought us all so close together, often short staffed, we needed to help each other out, going above and beyond our roles.

The journey north had now begun, and our first stop was Birmingham, where Ray had a day's work. From there it was on to Manchester to my parents' home, where we would be staying until we found our own place. Another bedroom, another air bed, little did we know we'd be waking up in the middle of the night on a deflated air bed several times. We had to laugh at our situation, and we did - many times.

Ray & Michelle

When we think about this period of our lives, we still feel a sense of anger. Anger that the 'powers that be' can come along and literally pull the plug on you. We are proud of ourselves, for the way we overcame our difficulties together. We supported each other throughout, with a true understanding and appreciation for each other. Leaving Shady, daughters and sons and going our separate ways, not knowing where we would end up, wasn't easy at all. We could have folded, broken down and come to a screeching stop, as a result of this experience, but we chose to stay and see it through. We've never been quitters and we have a resolute determination. We are so GLAD (pun 100% intended) we chose to stay, never halted our creative purpose of sound and vision, and took a leap of faith into the unknown. Nothing will stop us from creating. It's our purpose and no one will ever switch our purpose off.

DEDICATION

This chapter is dedicated to our close family who were there for us throughout this time. Also, a special dedication to our dear friend Trina Lomas who showed us great support at the time, as we were going through this experience and has continued to support us in our creative purpose. Additionally, we want to offer our immense gratitude to Rebecca Adams for the opportunity to share our powerful account and her phenomenal mindset encouragement, always.

Ray Coates

Ray Coates is a Singer-songwriter, poet, actor, international bestselling co-author, public speaker, and Father of 5. He is passionate about inspiring others to find their own unique voice by connecting through creativity. After losing his voice for an entire year in 2008 Ray released the single 'The Voice Within' to raise funds and awareness of head and neck cancer. https://music.apple.com/gb/album/the-voice-within/875761249?i=875761255

Due to this experience of disconnection and isolation as a result of throat cancer, Ray constantly reaches out to provide a voice for the voiceless. At the end of 2019 the song 'The Voice Within' was re-released, with a different version, to raise funds and awareness for the homeless prevention organisation Shelter.

http://itunes.apple.com/album/id1485352693?ls=1&app=itunes

Ray has also written music for a documentary series, aired on major networks in the USA in April 2020. In May 2020 Ray released his first album 'Garden of Life' for download
http://itunes.apple.com/album/id1500220066?ls=1&app=itunes

Ray has written a Song writing/writing program 'Song writing - Writing YOUR Unique DNA Songs' https://ray-coates-voice-songwriting-writing-your-unique-dna-songs.thinkific.com/users/checkout/auth The program is designed to help others open up their creative writing experience.

In 2020, Ray became an international bestselling co-author with the phenomenally inspirational book 'Smashing Through the Glass Ceiling'. Ray engages regularly in weekly creative connections through the following means:

* A weekly website Blog (including guest bloggers) e.g. https://www.raycoatesvoice.com/post/be-relentless-unstoppable
* A weekly YouTube Vlog 'Diary of a Songwriter - Let's Connect'. https://www.youtube.com/channel/UCdk2RObf3eVPtkQq6H_yugw

Ray has written a number of personalised 'DNA signature songs' and collaborates in joint song writing. The album features songs inspired by and written with 3 of the co-authors of 'Smashing Through the Stop Sign of Life': Track 7 - Rebecca Adams - 'Keep Going Always'. Track 9 - Susan Anne Lynn - 'Be Like This Child'. Track 11 - Michelle Roche - 'Altered State'. 'Garden of Love (Connecting IN Creativity)' is available to order on CD from Ray's website and is available from ALL major digital download stores, including iTunes http://itunes.apple.com/album/id1576506329?ls=1&app=itunes

WEB LINKS:
Website: www.raycoatesvoice.com
Facebook Business Page:
https://www.facebook.com/RayCoatesVoiceSingerSongwriter
Facebook Personal Page: https://www.facebook.com/ray.coates.129
Instagram: https://www.instagram.com/raycoatesvoice

Michelle Roche

Michelle's career began many years ago in the caring profession, working in childcare and then for the NHS for 25 years in total. However, art and crafts has always been her passion in life. This became even more apparent after recovering from a brain haemorrhage in 2012/2013. You can read her chapter in 'Smashing Through The Brick Wall' compiled by the amazing Rebecca Adams.

When Rebecca heard about Michelle's health scare, she asked her if she'd like to become a co-author and write about her experience. The book became a number one international bestseller on Amazon.

Michelle has always been interested in energy healing and natural remedies. In 2007 she became a Reiki practitioner; she also has a Diploma in Indian Head and Thai Foot massage. Painting is another one of her passions and she gets much of her inspiration from her partner Ray, a singer/songwriter. Listening to Ray craft a song inspires Michelle to create visual content, which then develops into a painting. Michelle has created the artwork for Ray's albums and for many of his singles too.

Their creativity combines beautifully together, giving vision to sound. Michelle has even written a song featured on Ray's latest album, Garden of Love (Connecting in Creativity) and she also created the artwork for the album cover.

Michelle's experience in life so far, has led her to where she is today - a business owner. U-gift was born in April 2021 and is a member of the chamber of commerce. Bespoke gifts of sound and vision for everyone to experience and enjoy. Ray and Michelle thought it made perfect sense for them to combine their skills and create gifts for all occasions. Card making has been a favourite hobby of Michelle's for many years. Personalised handcrafted cards come with each of the gift packages and can also be bought separately.

Michelle's other interests include, writing short stories and poetry, being out in nature and learning about the use of herbs to enhance health and well-being.

WEBLINKS:
FB personal: https://www.facebook.com/michelle.roche.5602
FB wall: https://www.facebook.com/U-gift-101666062008074/
Website: https://www.u-giftsoundandvision.com/
Instagram: https://www.Instagram.com/michelle.roche.5602
E-mail: u-gift365@gmail.com

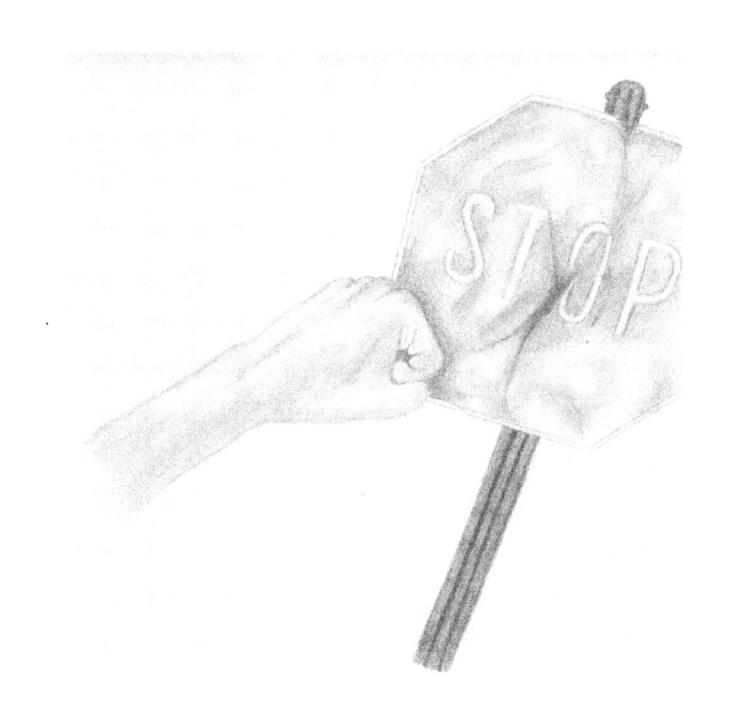

"With a kind heart and a strong mind, your opportunities are limitless"

Sherry Cannon-Jones

The Power of the Whisper in your Soul

The first time I physically felt emotional pain from observing the suffering of others, was when I was 18 and on holiday in Turkey.

Despite being very ill as a child and battling more than once to stay alive in the world as a baby, I consider my childhood to be one of stability, love and what most people would class as 'normal' - whatever that means. My parents were still together, and I had 4 siblings. The older three having got married or joined the Armed Forces, by the time I was old enough to have memories.

I grew up feeling loved and secure in my family and the world around me. I was confident and enjoyed life to the full, often pushing myself physically, which frustrated my Mum as she still thought somewhat, I needed a layer of cotton wool.

I already had a sense that life had a purpose in store for me. That I somehow would make a difference in the lives of others. Why else was I still here after nearly losing my life so many times?

On one occasion my parents told me the story of how many times they had been told I would not make it to a particular birthday and yet I kept going. And finally, they were told I was on borrowed time …. (Not bad for 52, eh?) I can still remember thinking "If I am still here, then it must be for a reason".

As a young girl my dreams were of getting married and having a family. I loved being around younger children way back then and I dreamed of what I wanted to do if I was to work. I wanted to be a Nanny or a Teacher. Funny how life turns out, I ended up on a management scheme for John Lewis!!

I have no idea how or why this happened other than it fitted in with the 'sensible choice' perspective… I had met my first husband at the age of 13 and got engaged at the age of 16 and so the options of, Nanny, Teacher or Tour Rep all seemed the wrong choice for different reasons.

Being a live-in Nanny meant I would be restricted in my ability to spend time with my fiancé. The path to being a teacher was too long and going to university didn't fit in with OUR plans and being a Tour Rep (something that wildly appealed to me), was not well received by anyone - parents or fiancé … ummm. So, I took the sensible option and joined John Lewis.

I married at 19 and then proceeded to move around the world with my husband who had joined the RAF. I would find a job wherever we were posted and although I enjoyed them all, what I failed to see was that I was actually losing a little bit of myself, piece by piece as the direction of my life became controlled by others. I digress…

As I said at the beginning, the first time I experienced being what I now know to be an empath, was on holiday in Turkey at the age of 18. My fiancé and I were walking along the road, and we stopped at a shop to buy an ice cream. As we exited the shop, there in front of us was a young boy aged about 6yrs old. He had no shoes on and his feet were dirty, as was his clothes, hair, and face. As I unwrapped my cornetto type ice cream and placed the wrapper in the bin, the young boy reached out a hand towards the ice cream, which I lifted out of his reach and followed my fiancé as he walked away.

All this happened very quickly, in the space of seconds but for me the whole concept of time slowed right down. Although by now, I was a good few paces away from the young boy, each step had felt like a dead weight and there was an aching in my heart that felt like complete sadness. It stopped me in my tracks and as I was holding my partner's hand. He stopped too and looked at me to see what was wrong.

Tears were flowing down my cheeks as I tried to get the words out that I didn't need this ice cream and yet the little boy most certainly did. I had literally felt his longing and then disappointment as I had moved along. With my partner looking at me as if I had gone crazy, I went back to the boy and handed him my untouched ice cream along with some money. The whole occurrence must have only taken a few minutes, but it deeply affected me, and I was somewhat shaken by it for a while after.

At 19 I really wasn't aware of what an empath was and for many years I moved through life being affected emotionally by different things. I saw where people were suffering. It was as if I was feeling their pain and their sadness, and each time I became more aware of the thought "I need to be helping, I am here to make a difference". I had no idea what all this meant and actually paid little attention to it once each incident had passed.

At the age of 27 I graduated as a teacher, finally having made some choices for myself, and following what I felt called to do. I loved it. Teaching is my passion and for 21 years I was privileged to have a helping hand in making a difference in the lives of the children I taught and their families. But still there was this nagging voice, this recurring thought - this is not it, there is more to fulfil.

When 9/11 happened, I was a single mum of two beautiful boys. Our marriage of 13 years had come to an end and to be honest, my confidence and self-worth were on the floor. My childhood dream of being married and raising a family together was in tatters and having the children part-time was becoming a reality as they spent every other weekend with their dad. It was at this time that I had renewed my Christian faith and was attending church.

In response to the devastation of 9/11, our church was sending out a group to help in the soup kitchens and aid centres and I knew it was something I wanted to do, but when I asked for help with childcare I was told, "What difference do you think Sherralyn Paget is going to make?" I was crushed!!

In that moment, I questioned who I was and my worth. "Why was I here?"

He was right. Who was I to make a difference?! I did not get to help and so began the dimming of the light in my soul. Its purpose and bigger mission quietened, while I got on with loving my life with my boys and making a home for them.

Two things happened at that moment in time. Firstly, I unconsciously set out on a path of allowing others to control my direction in life. I allowed my choice to be taken away, leaving me feeling disempowered and I began to doubt my ability to do what was right for me and my boys. The second, my soul started to become buried. Layer upon layer of other people's expectations, attitudes, actions and pressures, year after year until its voice was so quiet, I could barely hear it at all, except for those moments when I would see someone in need or vulnerable and my heart would ache and the need to help them would be overwhelming.

Yet sometimes I did nothing, for fear of being questioned by those around me. You see, if I gave to a homeless person, I would face questions and remarks from those I was with. I would hear remarks like, "Charity begins at home" and "How come you are giving our money away when we don't really have much?"

Life carried on very much this way until I lost my mum. It was like a sledgehammer!!

I was knocked completely off my feet. My world crumbled and suddenly, I was a 10-year-old girl feeling lost without her mum. For a while I ceased to function and sank into the darkest place I had ever been. It was the one and only time I just wanted life to stop. I truly wanted out and just not to be here anymore.

But my soul had other ideas. It had been knocked back into life and it was calling to me. Whispering that I still had so much to fulfil and now was the time to move my life forward and make a difference.

There was a fundamental shift. The desire to do something to make a lasting difference was burning strong, but I had no idea what it meant in real terms. I volunteered with outreach programs at church, made food hampers at Christmas for those in need, donated consistently to food banks, set up direct debits to charities and set aside money on holiday to give away to those in need… but as the months went past, I still felt like there was more that I should be doing.

As I began to become part of the online space, I saw that lots of people 'gave back' by supporting or setting up charities and so the thought of setting up a charity using my coaching business was born and that was 18 months ago. But something didn't feel right. I knew I wanted to set up a charity to make a difference in the lives of others but that was as far as I could get. I was continually thinking, "When I have a six-figure income, I will be able to set and fund the charity".

It was always a case of 'when I, when this happens, when, when, when!!' Until one day I was talking with God in utter frustration about the lack of clarity and momentum.

The response …. "You have got it the wrong way round… GET ON WITH IT, set it up NOW!"

It was as clear as day. I needed to get on and sort it out and start making a difference now on whatever level I was able to, and the rest would follow. And so, The Inspirited Fighter Foundation (TIFF) was brought into existence. I was elated. I thought that all the obstacles, the procrastination, the feeling stuck would vanish into thin air!!!!

Oh, my word! How I smile as I remember that thought. After walking around on air for a day, I came crashing down to earth the next day. As I sat down excitedly letting my thoughts and ideas spill out onto the page, I was gripped by a huge sense of overwhelm. I snapped and shut my notepad, fear ran down my spine and a loud voice shouted in my head, "THIS IS TOO BIG, YOU ARE NOT CAPABLE".

What was I thinking? I couldn't do this. There was way too much legal stuff to navigate. Why would anyone want to be a trustee? What did I know about fundraising? All these doubts and questions swirling around inside my head. It was a struggle to see that I could do this and so again I found myself in a state of procrastination, doing anything BUT what I needed to do to move forward with bringing the charity into existence. Bamboozled by the amount of legal stuff and paperwork, I stopped.

I believe, as do countless others, that we are guided by a power far bigger than ourselves. For me it is God, and the inner voice. The soul is my communication with God through the Holy Spirit. So, the repeated voice in your head we call our conscience is God. The chance meeting with a random person we view as coincidence is God. The gut feeling we call intuition is God. And so it was, time and time again, I would hear a voice. I would have a conversation with someone or see something in a book or online, all things bringing me back to the Foundation until I could no longer deny my purpose and I took the first step in making the foundation a reality.

I researched online about the process, the pitfalls, the legal bits, and I gathered information from anywhere I could find it. Who knew there were so many different organisational structures to choose from for non-profits? Just choosing this was a feat. Then came, the mission, the vision statements, and the objectives, what we would do and how we would do it.

As much as I felt I was making progress, the doubts and insecurities were still trying to take hold, so I took decisive action in order to put the Foundation out into the Universe. I created and launched the Facebook Page and set my intention so people would know who we are and what we intend to do. I also created and purchased some business cards. These two small action steps made such a difference. There was something tangible, something I could show my subconscious was real and had a purpose.

The Inspirited Fighter Foundation (TIFF) was born. The Facebook page is set up and running and the following is growing. I was keen for it to be making a difference from the get-go and so I signed up to the "Sponsor a room scheme" with Centre Point. This is to show the foundation is working towards its mission of helping to support those in need from the start.

Our mission is: Supporting the vulnerable with Homelessness, Hunger, Poverty and Mind Health.

Our vision is: To create a world where every human has shelter, food and dignity, eradicating homelessness, and poverty from our society.

Through donations and fundraising we will be able to provide the vulnerable and those in need with practical support, access to resources, guidance, and counselling, giving everyone we serve the opportunity to create a positive future for themselves. By the end of 2021 the aim is to be providing hot meals through our food hub and the 5-year aim is to have a local accommodation building to bridge the gap between Taunton and Weston-Super-Mare.

There is still so much to do and still a long way to go before TIFF will be operating in its own right and working on its own objectives, but I keep reminding myself, one step at a time. It is a huge process and I still get daunted, but I will not let it stop me. I get times where I am full of doubt and easily could give up, but I won't.

If you truly want something in life, you need to go for it. Yes, there will be obstacles. Yes, there will be challenges, but we are awesome human beings, and we can do anything we set our minds to, so it is onwards and upwards.

My message to you dear reader is this; We were all born with our own unique set of gifts and talents and our own unique purpose in life. That purpose may change and grow as we move through this life. It is by going deep with and connecting to your soul that you align with, that which is your direction, your passion, the thing that gives life it's meaning. Know you are held by a source that is so much bigger than ourselves and is always working for our good. You have everything you need inside of you to access a life of joy and abundance. The key is to be connected to it. Take the first step, go on the journey, create the life that is found on the blueprint in your soul. Make the difference, be the difference, be better, be more, and most importantly BE YOU.

<u>Dedication to the four most important men in my life.</u>

My two boys Jackson and Louie - you always have been and always will be the reason I am grateful for each morning I open my eyes and am blessed to live another day.

To my husband, Scott, you showed me what it was to feel loved for who I am without judgement or expectation.

To my Dad Brian, you have been the rock throughout my journey in life. Thank you for your wisdom, guidance, support, and unconditional love. It is an honour to be your daughter and you have my never-ending love and gratitude.

Sherry Cannon-Jones

"Let the beauty of the everyday sustain you"

Sherry Cannon-Jones is the 'Soul's Purpose Strategist', helping women to live a life of Soul Centred Joy. She is a qualified Silent Counselling Practitioner, certified in life coaching and mindfulness and brings her unique faith-based coaching and Energy Release techniques together, to take you from feeling empty, deflated and without direction in this life, to one of truly living, grounded in inner love joy peace and fulfilment.

As a teacher for over 21 years, Sherry's passion centred around making a difference in the lives of children and since 2018, she has been working to make a difference in the lives of those who are searching for a way to live a life of love, joy, peace, and fulfilment. When we feel our spirit is broken or we are so tired of life that we run on empty and find ourselves in a state of numbness and apathy, it is a tremendously lonely place to be. Outwardly it may appear as if you have everything you need, but inside you feel like you are slowing dying ... truth is, that is exactly what is happening to your soul.

Reawakening our soul and reconnecting to our inner Divine, allows us to draw on the infinite supply of faith and spirituality that guides us to living a life we rejoice in. We were born with everything we need inside us to connect to a life of joy and abundance. Our soul is our guiding compass to a life built on love, kindness, integrity, and authenticity. You can access the strength to come through your challenges with peace and grace.

Living in Somerset with her husband, father and their two pugs Winnie and Winston, Sherry is able to nourish her own Mind, Body, and Soul daily as they walk on the beach and around the beautiful countryside. This is also where many of her conversations with God take place.

Sherry has a strong faith and her life's journey is guided by God through the Holy Spirit. She has come to believe that all the names and labels people give to the 'something bigger than themselves' all refer to the same thing. For Sherry, it is God, others will call it 'universe, source, angels, law of attraction, divine spirit' to name a few. Love and kindness are two words Sherry tries to live by each and every day, particularly as a mum to two grown up boys, who are learning to make their way in the world.

Sherry wishes you love and light on your journey and if she is called to be part of it, then she is so thankful that your paths have crossed. You can share your collective consciousness as people awaken to the beauty of the everyday. May you let that beauty of the everyday sustain you through your challenges.

WEBLINKS:

Website: https://www.sherrycannonjones.com
Facebook Page: https://www.facebook.com/Soulcentredjoy
Facebook Group: https://www.facebook.com/groups/Thecontentedwoman/

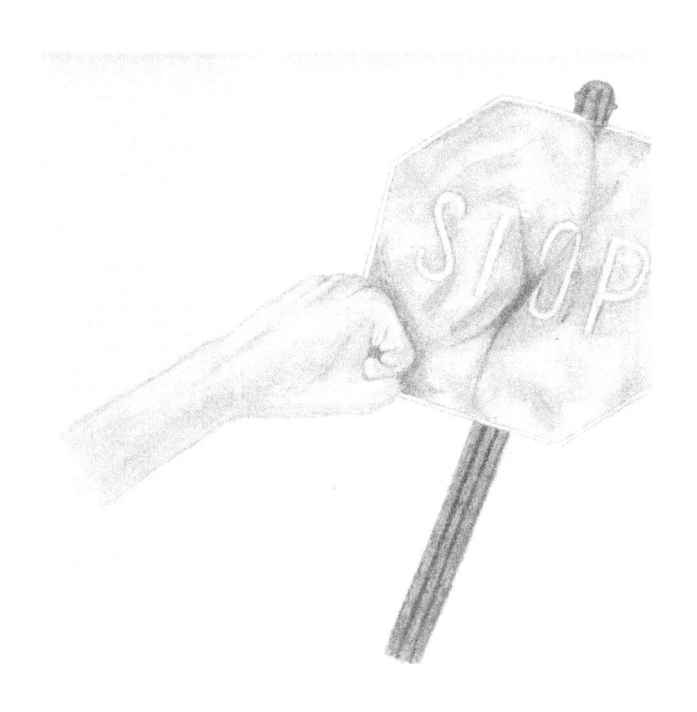

"Never let anyone or anything stop you from pursuing your dream. When things get tough, chin up and allow your passion to push you forward."

Julie Dickens

The Gift of Dance

"If you hit a wall, climb over it, crawl under it, or dance to the top of it."

For as long as I can remember, dance has been a part of my life. I can thank my mom for that. At the age of three, she enrolled me in my first dance at Kester's School of Dance in Weirton, Virginia. Little did she know, by her doing this, it would light a spark in my soul that would eventually lead to my life's work and legacy!

I don't really recall that first year of dance class. However, my mom told me how excited I was to go to dance class every week. I took tap and ballet, and I loved every minute of it. Especially the dance recital. And yes, my mom kept my first dance recital costume and my dance shoes!

At the age of 5, my family moved from West Virginia to Iowa because my dad had received a job transfer. One of the first things my mom did was to find a new dance studio to call home. I was so excited to get back to the dance studio and through dance I met friends in my new town. 'Shari Harris Dance' was a place of love, fun, exercise, friends, and family. Since we didn't have family in Iowa, my dance teacher and my mom became great friends, in turn became like family.

I took dance lessons with Miss Shari for 5 years and loved every minute of it. Unfortunately, she ended up closing her studio. It was such a hard time, but we ended up finding another dance studio to call home, 'Kathy Schutter's School of Dance'.

It was through my time here, that I became even more in love with dance. I was asked to be on the competition team which increased the number of classes I took per week. Outside of school, I spent lots of time at the dance studio. Miss Kathy became someone I looked up to. I remember thinking to myself that when I grew up, I wanted to have my own dance studio one day, like Miss Kathy. I had a journal where I began designing my own dance studio, "Julie's School of Dance".

I loved that through dance, it allowed me to spend more time with my mom. We would get time together in the car traveling to and from dance. We also got to spend time together when we would travel for our dance competitions. I remember one trip in particular, we got to travel to Chicago for a Tremaine Dance Convention and Competition. Mom and I had so much fun. We stayed in a fancy hotel, went shopping, ate at nice restaurants and enjoyed spending time together.

When I was going into 6th grade, my dad got transferred again. This time it moved us back east and we ended up in a small town outside of Pittsburgh, Pennsylvania. This was a really hard move and hard transition. I didn't want to move. I loved my house, my school, my friends, and my dance studio. Right away, my mom started shopping around for dance studios because she knew how important dance was to me. This time we ended up at 'Sandra Lynn's School of Dance'. I auditioned for the competition team and made the team. I was so happy to be back in the dance studio.

For me, my 7th grade year was one of the worst ever. When I started my new school, I got picked on. For some reason, a group of girls decided that they didn't like me because I dressed differently, I had an accent and I had long blonde hair. They threatened to cut my hair, they waited for me after classes, talked mean to me, shoved me and threatened to beat me up. I was devastated. I hated going to school every day. I even had to have a police escort to the middle school dance because they threatened to stab me at the dance!! Through all of this, dance became my outlet. I felt safe at the studio, I felt loved. Dance allowed me escape from the mean girls and the hurt. When I danced, I felt happy.

I continued dancing all through high school. I became really close with my dance teacher's daughter and spent lots of time with them. My dance teacher became like a second mom to me. I was asked to become a student teacher, which was my first job. I was thrilled and loved every minute of teaching. We took several trips to nationals throughout those years. One trip I will always remember was our trip to Ocean City, Maryland. I loved this trip because it was with my mom, my sisters, and my grandmother. We created so many memories on that trip!

When it was time to go to college, I wanted to major in dance, but my dad said no. I was upset at the time, but later understood his logic. My new home for four years became Radford, Virginia, where I majored in chemistry and biology and minored in dance. Dance, once again, became my escape and helped me relieve stress. It was the perfect balance for me. I loved going to the studio, taking classes, and shutting the rest of the world out. I also auditioned for the dance team and made it. I was so happy that I had the best of both worlds during my undergrad. My passion was being fulfilled.

After I graduated from college, I moved to Delaware where I began working as a chemical technician in a lab. Of course, just as my mom did for me years ago, I searched around for a dance studio. 'New Castle Dance Academy', under the direction of Valerie Gooding, was the studio I chose to call home. I began taking classes and soon became part of their amazing staff. I would work during the day in the lab and teach during the evenings. Valerie taught me so much about running a dance studio, how to interact with families and more importantly, how to be the best dance teacher. And just like all the other times in my life, my dance studio friends became my family. They supported me when life threw me challenges, advised me when I needed it, traveled to my wedding, and loved me. These women became some of my best friends.

I taught dance for 5 years with 'New Castle Dance Academy' while I continued my career in the lab. Being a dance teacher was so rewarding. From witnessing the little dancers walk into their very first dance class, to the older dancers mastering a difficult step. I loved every minute of it. I remember thinking to myself how rewarding it was to now be on the other side and once again, thinking one day I would have a dance studio of my own.

In 2001 I decided that I needed to make a career change. I loved being in the lab and my work was important, but I wanted to make more of a direct impact on others' lives, so I applied to an accelerated nursing program and got accepted. Unfortunately, this meant I would have to quit teaching dance. I was so sad, but I had to dedicate the next 18 months to this intense program.

After I graduated with a BSN in Nursing, from the University of Delaware, my husband and I moved to Texas for his job. I began my career as a nurse working 12-hour nights in the Neonatal ICU. I enjoyed my job, but for some reason I was miserable. I didn't have any friends, I was exhausted, and I missed dance. As I sat and thought about how it had been 2 years since I danced, I realized the hole in my life, the void. I needed to find a way to fit dance back into my life. And once again, I thought about how someday I would have my own dance studio.

Unfortunately, I did not make it a priority to fit dance back into life. Nightshift was kicking my butt, and on my days off I was tired and playing catch up. I took a few dance classes here and there, but it didn't fill the void in my heart.

In 2007, God blessed me with my daughter, Marley Paige. I was so happy to be a mom, especially a girl mom. And of course, I dreamed of the day she would be old enough so I could take her to her first dance class.

When Marley turned two, I began searching around for dance studios to take her to. I remember calling my mom and telling her the day had arrived. She was so excited and couldn't wait to see if Marley liked dance. The class lasted 45 minutes, and when she came out, she said she loved the class and wanted to go back! That was music to my ears! Over the next three years, I struggled finding a dance studio that was the right fit. I found studios that were too lackadaisical, too strict, studios that had no dress codes, studios that didn't have good techniques and studios that had terrible customer service. I kept hearing myself say, "If I had a studio, I would do this…"

In the spring of 2013, Marley was 5 years old and for several weeks, she came out of dance class upset. This alarmed me as a parent because dance should be fun at this age. I recall one night in particular she came out crying. My child did not cry easily. I had asked her what happened, and she said the teacher screamed at her because she went the wrong way in the dance. In that moment, I decided I was going to open my dance studio.

The time had come, and I began to get to work immediately. Right away, I started second guessing myself. Where was I going to find a building? How was I going to afford it? What if no-one comes? I could have let that negative talk get to me and extinguish my spark, but I was determined to make this work. I was determined to provide a happy place where children could learn to dance. I wanted to provide a place where they could come and make friends, to express their emotions, exercise and create memories with their families, just like I did all those years ago.

I had to get creative because I didn't have a lot of money saved up. I decided to start calling places that may sit empty at times like Yoga studios, churches, community buildings and karate studios. I didn't have much luck and started to feel defeated. Again, negative thoughts started to creep in. "This isn't going to work. I'm not going to find a place". I had a choice to make. I could give up or I could keep pushing forward! I decided to keep pushing forward and I finally got a "YES". Tracey, the owner of Yoga Balance, said she would love to help me get started with my dance studio.

I created my schedule around her schedule. She charged me by the hour to use her space. Was it the ideal space? No, but once again I got creative and made it work! My website was built, the schedule was set, the bank account was opened, the phone number was selected, and the fliers were created. Now, I needed to determine the name of the studio. For as long as I could remember, the name was going to be 'Julie's School of Dance'. For some reason, that wasn't sitting well with me. My mom and my daughter really played such an important role in bringing this studio to fruition. I wanted them to be a part of it, so I chose "JDM School of Dance". (Julie, Dottie, Marley).

In July 2013, I held my first dance class at "JDM School of Dance". I was so happy to finally have my dream come true. I was a dance studio owner! I opened the studio with about 20 students, but guess what? You have to start somewhere. I loved those 20 students and gave 110% to them. As the months passed, I continued to enroll more and more dancers. June 2014, I had my first recital. I remember feeling so proud, fulfilled, and passionate after seeing my dancers perform. It was so important to not only have happy dancers, but to build a community. To create a culture of kind, loving, positive families.

Over the next three years, my enrollment grew. I was still doing everything. I was a teacher, the bookkeeper, the marketing manager, and the CEO. Things were going great until I got a call from Tracey, the yoga studio owner saying she needed to meet with me. She explained she wasn't renewing her lease, which meant, I need to find a new building for JDM. Of course, this news was hard to hear, but I had two choices. I could be upset and pout, or I could rise up and press forward! I chose to rise and press forward! I knew in the back of my mind, in order to reach my goals, we would need a building of our own. I knew I was about to take JDM to the next level! It was scary but, I faced my fears and did it anyway!

Finding a new home for JDM Dance was not easy. My realtor and I toured tons of spaces, but nothing seemed to be the right fit. They were either too expensive, not enough space, not the right area, or too small. Frustration set in as we were on a timeline. I continued to pray to God that He would guide me in the right direction. Soon, a property became available at 8404 Stacy Rd in McKinney, Texas. It was perfect! JDM Dance had found a new home.

Little did I know the journey to our grand opening would be a rocky one. Dealing with contractors, timelines and landlords became a huge stress. This process was eye opening on so many levels. I realized people don't do what they say they are going to do, they tell you things to appease you, and they straight up aren't honest. My landlord said they would pay for the studio build out and I could use their contractors. Unfortunately, this ended up being the worst mistake I could have made. Their contractor was constantly telling me one thing and doing another. He treated me like I was stupid. He didn't keep me updated and they weren't on schedule.

At one point, I called a meeting between me, the landlord and the contractor. I arrived at the studio and walked in to meet with the two gentlemen. I was surprised to see 5 men instead. In that moment, a part of me wanted to turn around and leave, but I told myself, "I am powerful, I am a woman CEO, and I will come out of that meeting on top!" And that is exactly what happened. I was not afraid to say what I wanted, fight for what was right and stand up for myself.

The construction was not done on the date that was promised. Disappointed, upset and frustration set in. I wanted to just quit. It had been a long 4 months and negative talk began to fill my head. A quote that always helps me is "if it were easy, everyone would do it". Instead of sitting around being upset, which gets you nowhere, I knew I needed to take action and that is what I did.

There is a church in the same plaza as the studio, so I reached out to them to see if I could use their space until our building was ready. They were so kind to let me use a space that was unoccupied. Was it the best? No. But did it give me the opportunity to start my classes? Yes!

JDM School of Dance opened the doors to our new home in August 2015. The space was perfect, and all of the students and parents made it beautiful.

Since opening at my new location, I have grown my studio to 380 students, a long way from my 20 that I started with 8 years ago (and it's growing daily). I now have an office manager, a bookkeeper, a social media director and 8 instructors. Our two studio rooms are running classes 7 days a week and we have a growing Performance Team. Plus, I am opening up another studio at a new location soon.

Over the last 8 years, I have had a lot of obstacles to overcome. From employees quitting without a proper two week's notice, to parents spreading lies on social media, to keeping a business running during an international pandemic. It would be easy to stay knocked down or even just give up and walk away. But I didn't let any of those things stop me. Why? Because the passion in my heart for dance and the love of my students and dance family is too strong. I will always keep moving forward!

1. Discipline
2. Friends
3. Escape/emotional outlet
4. Fun
5. Exercise
6. Confidence
7. First job
8. Family memories/trips
9. Mentors, Kathy, Sandy, Valerie
10. Experiences

"If you hit a wall, climb over it, crawl under it, or dance to the top of it."
Face your fears and do it anyway.

DEDICATION

To my mom and best friend, I'm so grateful you took me to my first dance class all those years ago. Because of you, I discovered my passion. You were instrumental in making sure that dance was always a part of my life.

Thank you for being my biggest cheerleader. Thank you for all the times you supported me and told me to keep going. Your belief in me has always given me the strength I needed to keep pursuing my dream - no matter what. I love you always and forever Mom!

Julie Dickens

Julie Dickens is the Director and CEO of JDM School of Dance, based in McKinney, Texas. She is also the owner of Doodycalls Pet Waste Removal Service. She has been in business for many years and is an advocate for health and wellness.

Julie has been featured in magazines, on TV Channels in the USA and her brand and business is expanding exponentially, into a second location for her dance studio empire, to continue to share her passion of dance with others in the community.

She is a proud Mom to her daughter and is also a Dog Mama to her golden doodle

Ella.

WEB LINKS.

Facebook - https://www.facebook.com/julie.roachdickens
Website - https://jdmschoolofdance.com/
JDM Facebook - https://www.facebook.com/JdmSchoolOfDance
JDM Instagram – https://www.instagram.com/jdmschoolofdance
Doodycalls Facebook - https://www.facebook.com/DoodyCalls-Pet-Waste-Removal-Service-of-Dallas-Texas-102987447332

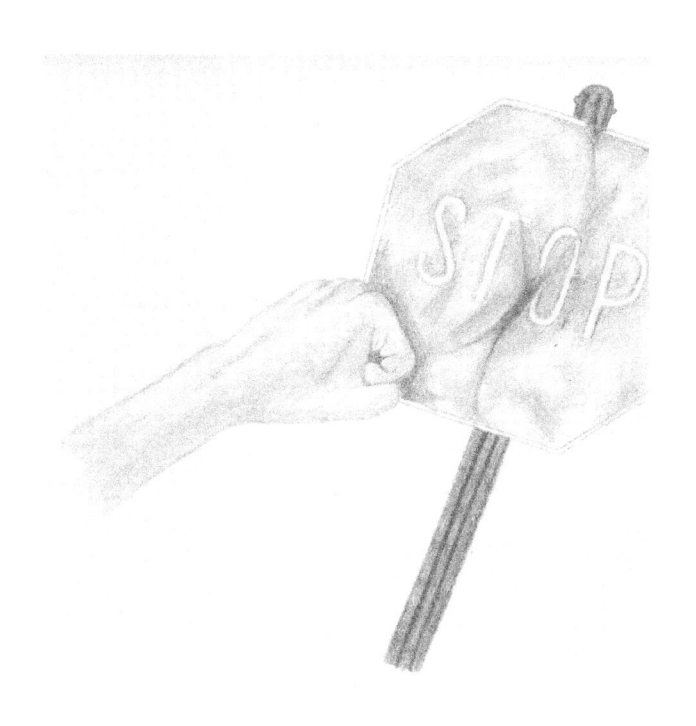

"Be like Tigger. Happy and bouncy and not letting things get to you."

Susan Anne Lynn

How many Hurdles does one have to take?

Have you ever thought; 'Oh no, not another hurdle to get over in life!'? and then asked yourself; 'How am I going to deal with this?', 'Will I cope?' or 'Will this be small or a much larger hurdle this time?'.

Now, what I call a hurdle, others may refer to as "a challenge in life".

I would think to myself, 'Okay Susan, you got over that one, but when will the next one be?' and then BOOM!!!, like clockwork, another would strike!!

This used to be the mindset I was stuck in for many years. Now, I look at every situation - be it good or bad, as a lesson to learn from and I'm grateful.

2008 was a year that I will never forget. I was about to face the biggest hurdle of my life and the smaller associated repercussive hurdles associated that would follow. After tackling lots in the five years prior, I started to believe that I did not have much strength left in me. I had dealt with a car accident whilst being pregnant, a house that was subsiding and unsafe; I vividly remember the cracks being so vast that I once awoke to a bird fluttering around my bedroom. I had split with my partner of my baby whilst pregnant amid a stressful house move, leaving my friends and the area I had known and grown to love (the area my son grew up in). His friends, school and life were there. Our life was there. The move was out of necessity, for my family, not choice.

Late 2003, alone, I had to pack my house up at the very latter stages of my pregnancy. I would eventually move eight days after giving birth (a week before Christmas). The birth was horrific, perhaps due to stress, but largely because my poor son was born with the cord wrapped around his neck. I will never forget the terrified look on the midwives' face. Her expression as she struck the panic button as my son birthed purple, is something I won't forget. Fortunately, my beautiful son was healthy, but little did I know I would face similar challenges again in just three years. I would also face this pregnancy having split with the father, and the birth suffered a similar fate with my next son also facing the cord around his neck. Both sons would later be diagnosed with being on the Autistic spectrum.

Fast forward again to 2008, having faced five years full of obstacles, I finally thought life was giving me respite. BOOM!!! The biggest hurdle yet awaited me. This one would give me the realisation of just how strong I am. How strong as humans we all are, or all can be. This hurdle initially made me want to curl up into a ball and let life pass me by but I, from somewhere, found the inner strength we all have within.

It had been a particularly hard year. We lived in a small 2-up-2-down council house. I was sharing my bedroom with my two youngest boys, whilst my eldest had the other. My son's autism would keep me up in the night, leaving me black eyed through sleep deprivation. I was seriously tired and unwell. Fighting each day for a wink of sleep, mentally and physically drained. Still to this day I am amazed my body fought on. My son's (my world) kept me going.

I had to do it all over again. We were moving again. Now classed as overcrowded, we were to move based on medical groups when a property became available. This time I had to consider the demands and needs of a young autistic boy; 'Could he escape easily?', 'If he did escape, could he disappear out of sight quickly?', 'How dangerous are the roads?', 'The parking – is it close enough to the house for me to manage any shopping, an autistic boy and a young toddler?'. 'Is it too much change for a boy with autism?'. All these questions were swirling in my head consuming me, as the one thing as a parent we want to do is to always keep our children safe.

Fortunately, we found the perfect location a stone's throw away from our previous house. This meant minimal change and my autistic boy would still be able to see the same park from his new house. This house was the one. I didn't have to worry about my boys being in danger daily. Whilst on the waiting list, unknown of whether or when we would be accepted, I would drive past the house and begin to manifest the move into existence. 'This is our house; you are the perfect house' I would speak.

In due course, the move came to fruition - this is the power of manifestation. The move dragged for what felt like an eternity, as the house was safeguarded to protect my autistic boy from escaping. It wasn't without support from my neighbour (who suggested this property) and our supportive social worker. For both, I am forever grateful.

I then got hit with the biggest hurdle of my life, to date. It was another 'Let's see how strong you really are!' moment. This would be something you never think could happen to you. 'It only happens to other people', I naïvely thought.

Well, a women's nightmare became my reality. I can picture the day clearly. I was expressing milk for my youngest son and found an unusual lump. I attempted to kid myself for 2-3 months 'It's just a blocked duct' I repeated to myself. 'It will go away', but the lump never did go away. I was only fooling myself. I had not told another soul. Deep down I knew what it was, perhaps I was just too afraid to face reality. I still remember the feeling of anxiety and dread raining down on me which was when I finally plucked up the courage to face the doctors. During the examination, I still tried to tell myself it was just a blocked duct, but my gut did not allow it. I knew the fate that awaited me. On examination, the doctor did indeed suggest it could be a blocked duct, prescribing a prescription of some kind, but to err on the side of caution would book me to be seen at the breast clinic. I still knew in my heart of hearts it was "the big C".

The appointment arrived at my door so quickly I didn't have time to think or process the impact of what might be. My head was all over the place. No parents around, as my Mum had long been passed and my father was 200 miles away. My neighbour stepped in and attended the breast clinic with me, and I could not have conquered this hurdle without her.

The day of my appointment I felt so sick and drained. We arrived at the breast clinic, and I was told to take a seat in the waiting room which was full of people. The wait was ominous. My mouth was getting drier with each minute that passed and my stomach was doing somersaults like a gymnast. I still recall the look on all the women who left the consulting rooms as I waited. The first lady seemed pleased – it must have been good news. Another left crying – she must have had terrible news. News she feared. I told myself 'You will not be one who cries.' I was so caught up, head running 100mph, my name was called repeatedly without realisation, until my neighbour tapped me and muttered 'They are calling you, Sue'.

I stood up on legs that felt like jelly. Every step towards the consulting room got harder and harder. The walk felt like agony. At the brink of throwing up, as I knew in my gut what news awaited me, I took a second and whispered to myself 'Come on Susan, pull yourself together'. I took a few deep breaths and then continued the walk.

The doctor explained to me about how he was going to take a biopsy. It sounded so painful. I feared the size of the needle. I could already feel the pain. I laid down and wished for it to be quick. I was sent to get a mammogram and a scan. I had never had a mammogram previously, so was nervous of what it may consist of. My breast lump was squished agonisingly in the machine. 'Deep breaths', 'you can do this' I repeated to myself. Next it was a long anxious wait. I waited, and waited and waited some more… My monkey brain growing with every second. I was still told it may be a cyst, but in my gut, I knew this was not the case. I was preparing myself for the worst and would eventually have to come back for another biopsy later. After another excruciating wait, the dread of what loomed over me growing. I returned for a second biopsy and was told what no-one wants to hear; 'The results show you have cancerous cells'.

I can't remember much of what was said that day. All I do remember is when I came out of the hospital I looked up into the sky, pointed and said, 'I'm not ready to go yet and I'm not going anywhere'. My boys would give me the strength to get through this. I thought 'how am I going to tell my boys?', I couldn't bring myself to tell my youngest two as they wouldn't understand. I told my eldest, who really didn't handle it well and went off the rails. I wish I had given him more support or asked for help for him. I'm so sorry for this and I'm so grateful that he is now in a good place and has forgiven me.

My appointment came to see the consultant at the cancer clinic. Once again, grateful my neighbour came with me. I was thinking 'okay if I have to lose my breast, I can take that, that's okay, but I can't lose my hair'. On reflection, I think this was because I thought everyone would stare at me. Sitting in the waiting room, I looked around and I remember the realisation that cancer would attack anyone. The illness did not discriminate… Old, young, white, black… male or female, it did not matter.

I noticed I was one of the youngest in the room. I never thought of it as a battle with Cancer. I made sure to look at it as any other illness. I was just seeing a doctor to get treatment, then I would be on the mend – there was no other option in my mind. The consultant called me in, again, I felt sick and my legs like jelly. The unknown was unnerving but the known was imminent. It was an aggressive form of cancer – I would need the lump removed, chemotherapy and radiotherapy. I was due to have my lump removed a few days before Christmas. 'I can do this!'.

My autistic son loved to jump on me and cuddle me, so I had to get his school to do a social story to explain that mummy was having an operation and would be sore. He could still have cuddles but couldn't jump. This was such a hard time for me being a single mum. My youngest went to stay at his aunties for a week which meant he had Christmas there and I only got to see him for a few hours that day. I was mentally and physically exhausted and just wanted to be fit for his birthday so he could be back home. I ensured I was, and he did.

I went back to the cancer clinic and saw the consultant. He was satisfied the lump had been properly removed but did mention I lost some lymph nodes. I was told there was a chance I could get Lymphedema and advised on actions and precautions I needed to take in order keep the risk low. This was worrying but it was a small price to pay. My body was given the opportunity to just about recover from the surgery then BOOM!! I was hit with chemotherapy. Six treatments every three weeks.

While waiting for my chemo, the council got back in touch with me to say that my house was nearly ready. It was going to have a kitchen fitted and they were going to send somebody out to me so I could look and decide which flooring and units to choose. This gave me something nice to think of which was good for this next stage of the fight, knowing that we'd be able to move into this lovely house and hopefully it would be ready. I was just glad the boys would have a nice place to start, in a bigger house with a big garden. I hoped things would go smoothly, but life never works out that way.

Yet again I had to do another social story for my son, to let him know that mummy was going in to have some medicine. We called it 'yuck-yuck medicine' because I couldn't really explain to him what chemotherapy was. He just wouldn't have understood and of course, I didn't want to make him upset.

The day of my first chemo arrived, and I really did feel uneasy and nervous, scared thinking of what was going to happen. So many different thoughts ran wild in my head – 'How is it going to work?', 'Will it hurt?'. I remember the pre-check blood tests before and agreeing to try the cold cap for prevention of hair loss. The rest of the pre chemo preparation is a blur. Again, sat waiting for the therapy felt like an eternity. I looked around and felt sorry for every other individual in the room. You don't know their story, what they've been through or what they're going through. There was some solace in knowing I wasn't fighting this alone, there were others who knew how I felt.

'Susan' was called. As I walk into the treatment room, all I could hear was 'beep, beep, beep' from the other patient's machines. I will never forget seeing so many people with drips going into their hands. It began to hit home, the fate that awaited me. I was given a seat and she explained to me how the cold cap would work. It was this big heavy brain freeze inducing helmet. My treatment lasted for three hours that day because of the cold cap. I can still feel the experience of having all the different injections pushed slowly into my veins. It all had to be done precisely and at the right temperature.

I was so grateful to have the care support package, where a carer would come to my home to help feed and wash the boys. In addition to helping around the house with the hoovering etc, these little things and the help meant so much to me. The night of my first chemo, I just wrapped myself in my bed feeling so ill thinking 'Oh my God - my head, mouth, head, nose…' It was all so painful. I was certain this was all side effects from the cold cap. If this was night 1, I was worried for the remaining nights so decided and told myself 'That's it, I don't care if I lose my hair now - I cannot carry on with the cold cap. It's too much for me'.

Words can't describe how much this initial treatment took out of me. For two weeks I could barely get out of bed. It such a struggle and my poor youngest one had to stay in the cot quite a bit because I just couldn't carry him, or if we came downstairs, he tried to leg it upstairs. I wasn't quick enough to get to him because I was just so drained and so tired as I couldn't stomach much. I was living off one meal a day as I only had the strength to cook once.

Two weeks passed and I was feeling a little better. I wouldn't say anywhere close to 100% but a little bit more like myself. My other autistic son had been away for two weeks at my nieces as they looked after him so that I only had to focus on one child. One child could still go to school, and I could still get rest when I needed it. I was and am grateful.

The council finally gave me a date to move in. I couldn't move in on the initial date because it was on the cycle of my bad first week which would occur after every chemo. I had to wait again until I had a good week so I would have the strength to attempt to move. Moving brought its own stresses - having to pay for two houses at the same time, let alone being single and having to pack up everything on my own while being so weak. How I found the strength to move is unreal. I recall telling myself, it is time to really believe in myself and that anything is possible when I put my mind to it. I dug deep.

Lying in bed, I would whisper to myself repeatedly, 'Come on Susan, you can do this'. I would visualise my life in the future. I would visualise me and my boys playing in the garden together and laughing. I would visualise myself fit and well. Doing this meant I would really feel, and more importantly, believe that things would be okay. Anyone can achieve this if you really believe in what you want and trust in yourself that you are strong and will overcome the hurdles you are facing. Find that inner strength from within, it is there within everybody.

Halfway through chemo, my hair was falling out all over the place. It was so depressing. I finally got the courage to get the clippers to it, so I didn't have to see hair everywhere any longer. It felt like I had lost my identity and it took me a few weeks to finally find myself and accept my new look. On my third session of chemo, I was sick the second the nurse put the needle in. The nurse was shocked saying that the chemo hadn't had time to make me sick. The nurse said it's just psychological and I was given anti-sickness tablets but to no avail. In hindsight, I must have manifested the sickness myself from saying 'I'm going in for my yuck-yuck medicine' and as a result, I'm mindful of what I say and do. Mindful of the repercussions of negative manifestation.

On completion of my chemotherapy, I was informed that radiotherapy would be next. It would be after respite and when I was ready. The consultant told me, as the cancerous tumour resided in my left breast, radiotherapy there increases the risk of heart and lung problems in years to come. Just when you think nothing else could make you low! My heart sank, thinking of my boys and my monkey mind jumping ahead (running through every 'what if' worst case scenario again). I took the decision to have the treatment sooner rather than later and prayed that my future was going to be okay. In fact, I told myself it had to be. I had no choice. I had to be okay for my boys. I reiterated this to myself day in, day out, until it began to stick, and I believed it again. The potential repercussions from the radiotherapy pushed further and further back in my monkey mind.

The first radiotherapy session was one of the worst treatment sessions I had to withstand. Again, battling with the unknown and my mind, the anxiety crept in. I vividly recall the nurses having to get me aligned and perform the first dot tattoo as being a very unpleasant experience. Just like with the chemo, as the treatment went on, I became more and more tired, worn down. Attending the hospital daily became a chore. I can remember walking up the stairs and feeling like perhaps I should just crawl up them because my feet were that sore it felt like I was walking on bones. It is a strange feeling I hope to never experience again.

It's amazing how strong someone can really be when they need to be, finding that inner strength. We all have that strength. We just need to learn how to dig deep within us to find it. I have learned that my God, I'm so strong and I really can cope with a lot. I now say to myself 'you're like Tigger - you may get low from time to time but you're never low for long as you bounce up like bouncing Tigger'. I just say to myself I need to watch out I don't hit my head when I bounce.

I look back at what I called a hurdle and say thank you for the lessons. If the patterns keep repeating, I analyse my situation, ask myself 'What did I not learn from this hurdle?' and look again. Sometimes we don't see the lesson straight away, but we will do in time.

DEDICATION

I dedicate this chapter to my incredible boys who have taught me so much - I love you all so very much. You have been my light in my darkest days.

I also dedicate this chapter to my niece, Vickie, and her husband Steve for having one of my boys and showing him a good time and taking his mind off missing his mum and brothers when I was battling cancer. This truly did give me peace of mind to heal.

To my wonderful old next-door neighbour, for being such a great support to me the whole time I lived next to you. For being my rock while I was dealing with the big C.

Last but no way least, to the wonderful Margaret who came into our lives as part of her job, to help support me and my boys while dealing with the big C, and once that ended you still stayed in our lives. You became part of the family, and we all love you dearly.

Susan Anne Lynn

Susan is a single mum to three amazing boys. Born in Germany, she moved around a lot as she was an Army child.

She used to work as a care assistant for the elderly which she loved, as she loves to care for people. As a special needs mum, she has completed a lot of workshops and courses to help her understand her two boys' autism.

Susan is a committee member for ASD family help charity, after having their support over the years, she felt it was her time to give something back. She is a loving person and wears her heart on her sleeve. She also aims to always spread love around the world with a smile.

Susan loves to walk in nature and to be one with it. She finds peace while she does her meditations and she loves being in a group to do this, as she feels more loving energy. Susan had a spiritual awakening a few years ago which has set her on her new path, and she wants to learn all she can from energy healing and how this might be able to help the mind as well as the soul. Susan has her level 1 Reiki and is aiming to complete the level 2 with her master by the end of 2021.

During 2020 and 2021, Susan has felt her calling and it is to find a way to help teens with special needs who are suffering with mental health to find their inner peace. Also, to help their parents and give them the right tools.

She feels that she has been very lucky to have been part of writing some lyrics for an international song 'Our Connection' which came out in 2021. She also has another song 'Be Like this Child' which is out now and Ray Coates sings it beautifully.

WEBLINKS:

Facebook Wall: https://www.facebook.com/susan.a.larkin
Instagram: https://www.instagram.com/susan_soul_of_peace_and_love_/
Twitter: https://twitter.com/SusanSoulOfPeal

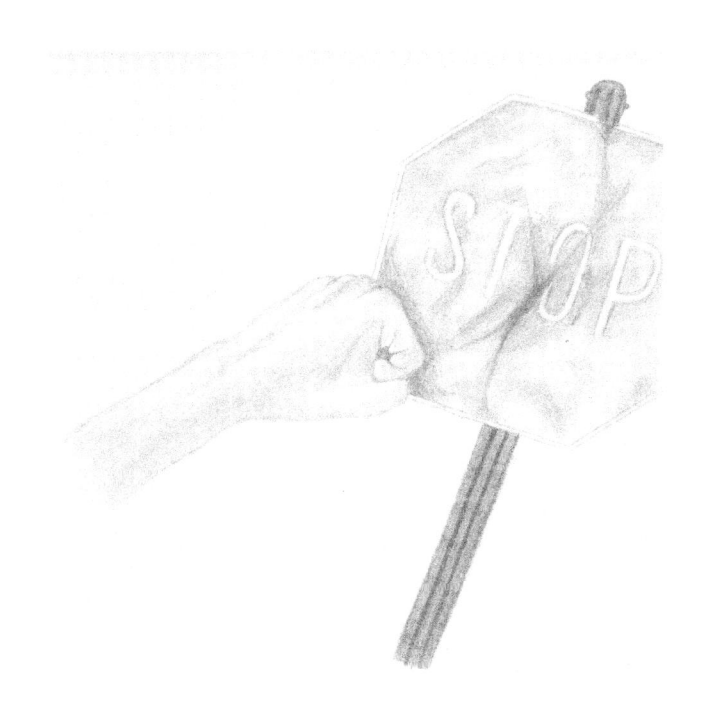

"Take the risk as it may be your best choice yet and if it's not, remember you tried".

Ashley Stanford

Letter Through The Post

I was going through my daily life as I usually would when, on the 10th of March 2017, the unexpected happened…

I received a letter through the post and opened it, which if you don't recognise the envelope or sender, you think it's important. It was a letter from The Salvation Army Family Tracing Service regarding a family matter and hoping that they had got the right person! I was confused and shocked as I was not aware of any family matters. It also threw me off a little as it had my old middle name printed on the letter and not my now given middle name.

I contacted the Family Tracing Service (The Salvation Army) by phone and was told that my biological Grandmother and my biological Father wanted to contact me. I was taken aback. With my initial response being complete shock, the tears streamed down my face, and I felt overwhelmed and overloaded. Never in a million years did I think this would happen!

I jumped to a lot of conclusions and thought of the why now's and the what if's.

My brain was asking so many questions I couldn't keep up with it. So many scenarios went through my head. What was going on? Was this serious?

The Salvation Army explained to me that my biological Grandmother wanted to speak and meet with me and so I was asked if I wanted my personal contact details passed onto the relevant parties. I felt quite anxious and nervous about what would happen as I did not know what to expect, but I agreed anyway as you never know, this could be my one and only chance of this ever happening.

So, they passed on my details, and very quickly (within approx. 10 days), I was contacted by my biological grandmother. We had a nice phone call asking each other about our lives and what we had done and been up to. She confirmed that she did want to meet me in person to see me. It felt lovely to be wanted by a member of the family I'd never met but this was all going a bit too quick. I needed a bit of time to think about this, so that my brain could process what was going on and the importance of it all. Yes, I was worried about meeting her as I didn't know her, and I also didn't know what to expect at all.

I did finally agree to meet her, but on my turf – in my hometown so that I would be much more comfortable. We met up in a lovely Italian café in Trowbridge, Wiltshire and I decided to ask my friend to come with me so that I wasn't feeling tense, and she could calm my nerves too. She agreed and we went.

We sat down and enjoyed a cup of tea together and we spoke about family, jobs, and lifetime experiences. Then she explained that my biological father wanted to contact me. I had got over the initial shock in the phone call we had had previously, so this news actually came less of a shock, but I still felt nervous about the whole situation. I agreed for her to give my contact number to my biological father.

We enjoyed each other's company for a duration of time and then as she left to go home, she just said "Bye, speak soon". No hug or anything. I did not know what to think. I felt all sorts of emotions on the way home, and I started to question whether I had done the right thing with meeting up with her or not.

I also wondered whether anything else would come from this meeting. Oh, how shocked I was at what I received next!

After this meeting, about a month later, I received a handwritten card (which was not even delivered to me). It was delivered to another family member from my biological grandmother. I opened the envelope, and as the contents of the card caught me off guard, I felt a whole range of feelings from being shocked and annoyed, to feeling offended and really judged. The contents of this card stated a few unnecessary comments.

To quote a small piece of it:

"We are a hard-working family, could you use some time even doing charity work or a part time job? We are never on the dole. This brings making you feel good".

Just by this quote alone, I'm sure you can imagine what the rest of the card contained.

I felt this card was very condescending and judgemental as my biological grandmother didn't even know me. Guess she judged the book by the cover when she met me and didn't even give me a chance to even explain my upbringing and what challenges I have faced and still face now!

Have you ever felt like that? Judged by someone who doesn't know anything about you? The saying is true "You never know what goes on behind closed doors" and that's the reason why no-one should judge anyone.

Now, during our meeting I had explained to my biological grandmother that I had some health problems going on that were being investigated, which limits me to what work I can do. So, the sentence above gave me the impression that she hadn't really listened to anything I had told her about my life, and this left me feeling upset and quite offended as *she* was the person who had looked for *me*. And, within an instant it was like I wasn't good enough for "her family".

With this being said, I felt like this was the final straw for this encounter with my biological grandmother. I did not need the negativity in my life, as this would only bring me down in the long run. I had a good chat with my friend regarding this and my friend was in agreeance with this decision.

When the Family Tracing Service contacted me, it was a risk that things wouldn't be all sunshine and puppies. However, it was a risk that I needed to take and unfortunately it was not a good one with my biological grandmother.

I was then contacted by my biological father, and we spoke on the phone for quite some time, which felt good, as I got to know him a bit before meeting him. We agreed to meet in person and again, I decided to meet in my hometown so that I felt comfortable. We met in a café, and it felt quite exciting, but I was so nervous at the same time. I mean, this was my biological father. His wife was coming with him so that added to my nerves I think too.

I felt a bit more comfortable when I met them both, together with my friend who I brought along with me, again for support. It went well and my biological father answered all the questions I had. It was great! I found out more information on the extended family I had, and I also found out why my biological father was not around for my life and what happened. That was, in itself, huge!

I was also informed that I had 3 other siblings that I did know existed but did not know much about them, and I have still never met, even to this day of writing this chapter. My biological father gave me some information on them on the 2nd time we met up. That was also where I learned I was an auntie as well. My biological father's wife is lovely and has taken this all very well. After this second meeting, we carried on messaging and had phone calls and we also carried on meeting in my hometown too. My biological father has always been incredibly open when it comes to answering my questions about everything and about himself and why he has not been in my life, which I feel is a good thing.

Now, as I'm getting to know my biological father, I do hope that he wants to and stays in my life and doesn't disappear. Meeting him was something I needed to do, to get some of the answers to the questions I've always wanted to know and that my mother couldn't answer. I also needed to do that and I'm proud of myself that I said yes to The Salvation Army Family Tracing Service because I would have always questioned it, as I live my life, if I'd have missed out on the chance to meet him and learn everything too.

I don't really remember when I was told that the man that was raising me was not my biological father, as I always thought of him as my dad, and didn't think any differently as no one else was around. I guess in a way I shrugged it off. It didn't really become real until the letter came through the post and we started to talk. Though I hadn't heard much about my biological father as I was growing up, I did know he existed. I didn't know where he was or whether he wanted anything to do with me.

Now, to take you back to my childhood and give you a bit of a background into my upbringing…

My biological father and his family have never been in my life since when I was born. My Mother had me at a young age and then met my Stepdad when I was 2 years old, and my stepdad took me on as his own and is still there for me and I am now 27, so I call him dad and my mum and stepdad have given me the best upbringing they could have, although life tests us and I was not easy at times, as I had my moments as a child.

My mother has always been open and honest with me about my biological father and his family which I couldn't be more thankful about. As for my Stepdad, the old saying goes; "Any man can be a father, but it takes a real man to be a dad". I could not have asked for any better 2 people to have raised me – My mum and

My Dad (stepdad) and I am forever grateful.

I wanted to write this chapter of my life to encourage people to find their biological family members or relatives. Even though they haven't been in your life, it doesn't mean they have not tried to find you. This could be the missing piece to your family tree. Whether this is a good or bad ending, you must believe you did the right thing in continuing the lead.

I took the risk and mine has had both a good and bad ending. I'm still in contact with my biological father every now and again, as he works a lot of hours and isn't always at home every night. Since relocating in 2020, I haven't managed to see my biological father in just over a year due to one thing or another, but we do still plan to meet up again and spend some more time getting to know each other.

I'm not sure where this will lead in the future but if one thing is for certain, I will just take it in my stride whatever happens.

This message is for you.... If you don't try, you will never know the outcome. Take the risk as it may be your best choice yet and if it's not, remember you tried.

DEDICATION

My Mum – Thank you for always doing your best for me, thank you for being you and keep being you! I will be forever grateful for everything you have done for me. All the times you have raised me single handedly, you are inspirational!! Thank you, Mum!

My Dad/Stepdad – Thank you for taking me on as your own daughter. It has and always will be appreciated and I'm forever grateful. Thank you for everything you have done for me! Thank You Dad!

Ashley Stanford

Ashley Stanford lives in Swansea, although she was born in Trowbridge, Wiltshire. She has been working in the care industry for many years and is also a published co-author in this book too.

Ashley loves music and gaming. Ashley's future goal is to develop the hamper part of the business and live a fulfilled happy life.

WEBLINKS:

Website: www.littlerubystreats.co.uk

Personal Facebook: https://www.facebook.com/Ashleyairlines123

Business Facebook: https://www.facebook.com/groups/lrtreats

Instagram: https://www.instagram.com/treatslittlerubys/

Linktree: https://linktr.ee/Littlerubystreats

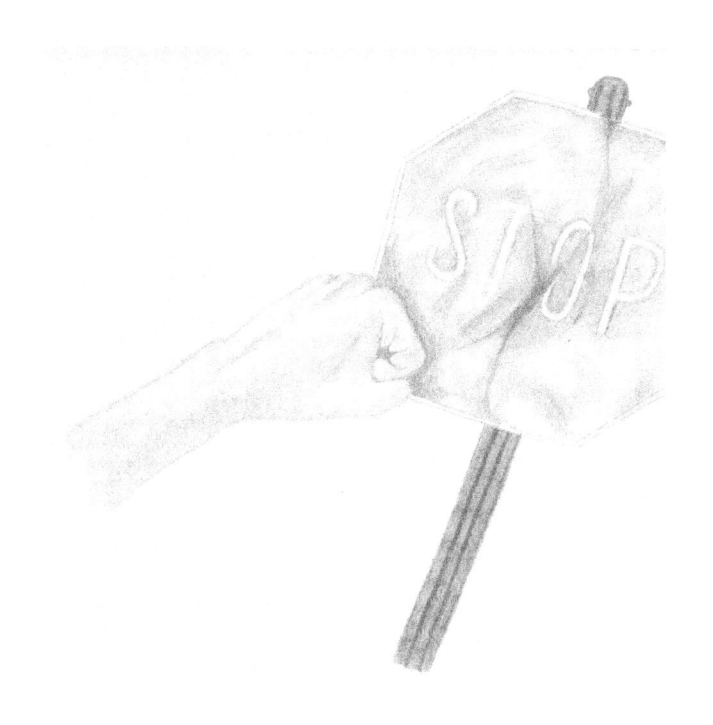

"Problems are inevitable, suffering is a choice. Stand up with courage and strength and know it will not last".

Louise McGough

My Journey To Motherhood

Growing up being a mum was the only thing I wanted. I had it all planned - I would get married, and we would have a boy and a girl and live happily ever after. But of course, life isn't that simple, and the universe put a couple of obstacles in the way!

Fast forward to 2001, at the age of 22, I met my soulmate Steve…unfortunately he was someone else's. My best friend's to be exact, but as a foursome with my partner at the time, we became great friends.

In September 2002, when both our relationships ended, we got together and on 22nd December 2004, we got married.

Starting a family was the next step, and we were delighted to find out that we were expecting in July the following year. We couldn't wait to tell my parents! Our joy was short lived though, as I started bleeding quite heavily and I was told I had an Ectopic pregnancy. I had no idea what that was, but I was told that I would need an operation. The egg gets stuck in the fallopian tube, and nothing can be done to save it. I discovered that it is quite a common condition but also life threatening if not operated on. So, the foetus was removed but my fallopian tube wasn't. It was just patched up, to give me more chance of falling pregnant again. We were heartbroken. As well as recovering physically for 6 weeks from the operation, emotionally the recovery was hard. Everywhere I looked I saw pregnant women, or small babies. We took some time to recover before deciding to try again.

In May 2006, I did fall pregnant again. Because of my previous Ectopic, I had to have an early scan. We were devastated to discover it was another Ectopic pregnancy. It was heart-breaking. This time when they operated, they took the tube away too. Having it patched up last time was probably the cause of the 2nd ectopic because of scar tissue.

This all took its toll on my already fragile mental health. It also affected Steve badly. He felt useless because I was the one dealing with the recovery in my body, and together we shed many tears. The one thing we both really wanted was to be parents. It felt so unfair that it wasn't easy for us. There were family members and friends of ours all having babies.

We have always been very open about other ways to become parents and we considered our options. There was no reason why we couldn't have a baby naturally, but I felt that I didn't want to put my mind and body through it again, and Steve felt the same. We couldn't face or afford IVF or surrogacy, but adoption really appealed to us.

We decided that would be the way we would proceed. But again, the universe threw obstacles at us, with Steve being made redundant and we had to sell our house, to clear debts etc. As it was, we had to wait a while to start the adoption process, as they must be sure that we had come to terms with not having a birth child.

We contacted our local Barnardo's in 2009. It was exciting, nerve-racking, and overwhelming. The process is incredibly invasive. Our social worker wanted to know EVERYTHING, and I mean EVERYTHING!!! From our childhoods to jobs, from ex partners to our sex life….it was all laid bare!

It was difficult to talk about, at times, and lots of emotions were brought to the surface. We never understood how relevant it all was. We also had weeks of workshops, where we learned about all the emotions a child would feel, and how we would help them, the kinds of special needs an adopted child may have.

The social workers running the workshops talked a lot about the 'backpack' adopted children come with. I remember the group we were in, had 3 other couples and a single woman. We used to gather in the kitchen at the break and used to chat amongst ourselves asking "Can It really be that bad?". From my point of view, and I'm pretty sure all the others on those workshops would agree, that yes, it can be that bad!

In the summer of 2010, we were officially ready to adopt. After sitting in front of a panel of people, our hopes, and dreams in their hands, they said yes! We had been approved to adopt a sibling group of 2, with either 1 of each sex or 2 boys, aged between 2 and 7.

I was taken aback by a magazine we were given called 'Be My Parent', which had pictures of all the children awaiting adoption. It was heart-breaking to see their gorgeous photos and read their little bio about them. We were sent a couple of profiles of children by our social worker. Both were boy siblings, the 1st one had the most gorgeous photo of 2 boys, but their profile didn't really appeal to us. The other profile was a real joy to read, but the picture of the boys wasn't the best. We always said we wouldn't go by photo alone, and that their profile was more important, and so we asked to proceed with the 2nd one. We remember our social worker being delighted. It was as though she knew they were meant for us.

Things moved really quickly, and we met with the boys' social workers to learn more about them. We met the foster carer, nursery teacher and paediatrician.

It was a surreal feeling, knowing that there were 2 boys out there who were possibly going to be our sons! Again, we had to sit before a panel of 6 strangers and discuss with them how we could meet their needs and why we were the best choice, and what we would do in certain situations etc. It was scary! We could do no more. After hours of interviews, paperwork and training, our future was in their hands.

We then had to wait to find out….

I can't remember how long we waited, but the phone call came on the youngest's 2nd birthday. We were busy decorating their bedrooms, in anticipation, when our social worker phoned. We were delighted to hear that we had got a unanimous YES at panel! We were going to be parents!! 6 years after getting married.

So, we looked forward to enjoying our last Christmas as a couple. We thought a lot about the boys on Christmas Day, wondering what they were doing, what presents they had been given. I emailed their Foster Carer that Christmas night and were told they had had a great day. They had been told the week before that they were getting a new mummy and daddy, and apparently the eldest was very excited about that! As were we! We busied ourselves getting their bedrooms ready and bits and pieces bought for them. We knew they didn't have much to bring with them and we wanted to make their bedroom and playroom as welcoming and lovely as possible for a 4-year-old and 2-year-old.

I applied for adoption leave from my job with the NHS, and we put a book and video together to send to the boys to introduce ourselves, along with a little teddy bear each.

We were to have 10 days of 'introductions', where we would stay close by to the foster carer's house, so the boys and us could get to know each other. We would travel to our hotel on January 5th, and we were to meet the boys on the 6th, after first meeting their birth father....it was going to be one hell of an emotional day! I'm not sure either of us got much sleep that night.

Again, obstacles were thrown our way.

Steve got stuck at work on the 5th of January, due to a bomb scare, and he wasn't allowed to leave the ward he was working on. My grandad had a stroke and was really poorly in hospital, and on the day we were due to meet the boys for the first time, I had a flat battery in my car!

The boys' social worker had to come to pick us up to take us to meet BF. It was incredibly painful to see this man who had tried so hard to parent his sons when their birth mother wasn't capable. He shared stories, hopes, and dreams with us. We all shed tears. It felt so wrong to have the excitement inside me that we were about to meet our sons, as he was giving them up. We had a photo together and went our separate ways. We then went to the foster carers house to meet our boys.

The memory of that moment is of 2 small blonde boys eagerly waiting at the glass door. The eldest holding a red balloon - his favourite colour even to this day. Much else of the following 7 days is a blur. We spent time with the boys at the foster carers, increasing in time every day, and being there when they woke, bathing them and putting them to bed too. We took them out to a zoo, made cakes, went to parks and it was exhausting!

The original plan of 10 days was shortened as everyone felt the introductions had gone well. We travelled back to our home on the 13th of January, leaving the boys with the foster carer. Then on the 15th of January 2011 our sons moved in with us. Another sleepless night had, excited for the day, two walking, talking, demanding little boys with their very own 'backpack' who were funny, resilient, and bloody hard work completely changed our life for the better.

Six weeks in, we had a visit from our Social Worker. She asked us how we were. 'Knackered' was our answer. She said to imagine parents with a six-week-old baby…. that's us. We were at the same stage of parenthood.

We set about making wonderful memories for our boys. We went camping and went to LegoLand. We travelled to beaches and went to CentreParcs. We found a mutual love for Cornwall, which has become a special place for the four of us.

10 years on we have been through a lot. Diagnoses of Autism, ADHD and Attachment issues plus school refusal and therapy. Appointment after appointment…. oh, the appointments!! Home schooling a child that has no interest in wanting to sit and learn and fighting for the right placements for him can be testing. But this is how it was meant to be. We had the job to be parents to 2 boys who needed love, care, and stability. People say how lucky the boys are to have us, but we believe we are the lucky ones.

We now have 2 teenage boys, who refuse to shower, tidy their rooms, or go outside! But who are also loving, funny, kind, and handsome. We couldn't love them more.

At the time we met the boys, Adele's song 'Make You Feel My Love' was playing on the radio constantly. These words to me are so apt….. 'When the evening shadows and the stars appear, and there is no one there to dry your tears. I could hold you for a million years, to make you feel my love.'

It will remain our family song always, although the boys are not keen on me singing it to them!

I never gave up hope of being a mum. My boys grew in my heart, not my tummy.

DEDICATION

I dedicate my chapter to the following people in my life....
Steve, my husband, soulmate, best friend, and the best Dad to our boys.

Charlie, my favourite 14-year-old, and Cain my favourite 13-year-old. I'll be forever grateful to you both for making me a mummy.

Mum and Dad for all the support and love you have given me throughout my life. To everyone who was part of our journey……you know who you are.

Rebecca for allowing me to be a part of this amazing book.

Lastly, to all of you for reading my chapter. I hope a part of it can help you if you have gone through the same experience.

Louise McGough

Louise is 42yrs, married and mum to 2 amazing boys. The youngest has Autism, ADHD and Anxiety. Working for herself is very important because of this, so she can be around for her son. She has a Network Marketing business, which she works with her husband of nearly 20 years.

Louise is a qualified Florist and has a love of gardening. She is passionate about British Grown flowers and grows her own cut flowers. Louise decided to turn her hobby into a business in 2021 called Grown & Gathered, combining her floristry skills and fresh cut flowers from her garden to create beautiful simple bunches. Her ethos is freshly picked, simply wrapped, beautiful flowers. Her client base is expanding.

Louise enjoys cooking and spending time with her family. Together they love visiting castles and stately homes. Cornwall is their favourite place to holiday.

WEBLINKS:

Website - https://www.grownandgathered.biz/
Facebook - www.facebook.com/louise.mcgough
Instagram - www.instagram.com/louise.mcgough_growngathered
Network Marketing - www.shopwithmyrep.co.uk/avon/lotuscosmetics

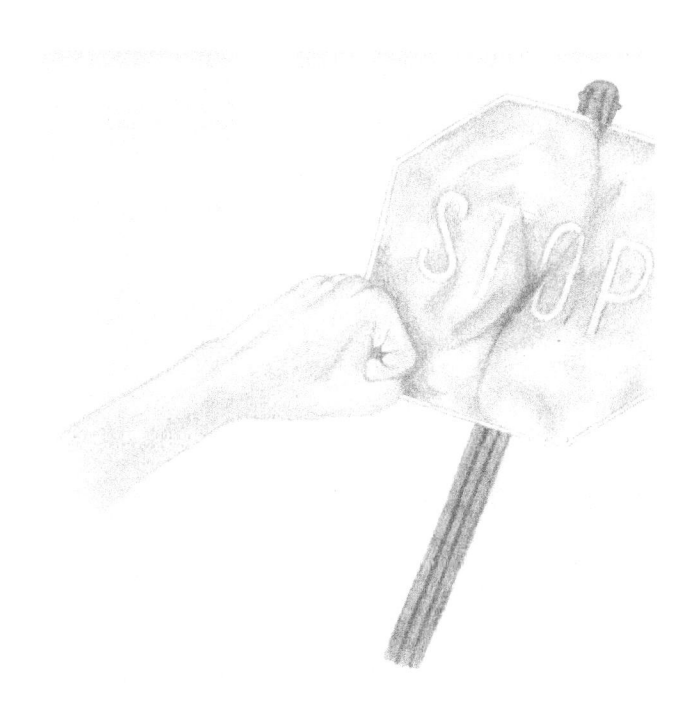

"Life can be uncertain but always believe you deserve the best".

Karlene Jordan

Never be Afraid to Start Over

A normal person from a little island in the Caribbean, this is going to be insane.

At 35 I became pregnant with my son. Now there were questions over his paternity, as I was a bit of a wild one, but nevertheless I continued with my pregnancy.

This pregnancy was far from the perfect pregnancy, as I suffered with pre-eclampsia which resulted in many hospital stays while carrying my most precious cargo. At thirty- two weeks, seven days after being in hospital for a week, the consultant told me that I had to have an emergency c-section. So, on Friday 26th February 2010 I was scheduled to have the emergency c-section at 8:30pm - I was nervous and worried. Anyway at 8:58pm it was all over.

Kwasi had entered into the world!

The day after his birth, I was told by the doctors that they had given him 48 hours to live! Those words pierced through me like a knife slowly cutting my heart out my chest.

On the Sunday after his birth, he stopped breathing and he went all blue. I thought that was it, "I've lost my precious cargo!". I started praying and asking God to cover him…… then suddenly, the ventilator made a noise – Kwasi was back. His first three weeks were spent in NICU (Neonatal Intensive Care Unit) on the ventilator with a tube in his chest, as he had a collapsed lung and they needed to inflate it.

Then the day came, Thursday 18th March 2010, when Kwasi was discharged. I was ecstatic, overjoyed, grateful and thankful. My precious baby boy was coming home with me, and I get to cuddle him and be his mum. I was grinning from ear to ear.

The day of Kwasi's baptism arrived. I was the only mum there without the baby's dad, but I was surrounded by the people I loved the most - my niece, Mickel, my best mate Maria (godmother), my other mate Marcus (Kwasi's godfather) and of course the other loves of my life - my daughters' Keniah and Kenyah. During the service I remember my niece whispering to me "Aunty, you're the strongest woman I know" which brought tears to my eyes, because she didn't realise that her aunt was battling with shame and self-doubt as I sat there listening to the priest speak and just wanted the floor to open and swallow me in.

After the service, reality stepped in that I was now a single mother of three children. Two daughters from my previous marriage and my son who is without his father figure in his life. But my life must go on…. "I've got to be strong for my babies".

Seeing that I spent time in and out of hospital, my maternity leave was split before and after Kwasi's birth and I was only left with three months after his birth to take time off work, so I asked my gynaecologist for another three months, extending it to August 2010.

I was now faced with returning to work to the gossiping, laughter, and insults by colleagues from my department and other departments. You see at that time; I was working for the water company in my home country, and I was based at the Head Office so I interacted with colleagues from various departments.

So, with my big girl underwear I strutted into the compound, head held high, smile on my face and I told myself "I'm going to kick ass no matter what was thrown my way".

As my years went by, my little miracle boy blessed me with a promotion, which I enjoyed tremendously. I was now an Accounting Technician II but due to the location I only did it for about four months as I would be late in collecting my children from the babysitter and that incurred additional charges and as a single mum with only one income it was a bit challenging.

So back to my substantive post I went, and I was happy with that, as I was more or less local to where my children were, so I was able to shoot off home from work with short notice if needs be.

A year after, who would have thought that my life would completely change?

The love of my life became a widow. This person I had loved since I was sixteen. He was and still remains, the kindest, sweetest, and most genuine person I know, besides my mother who is deceased.

We used to communicate regularly on Facebook as friends, just checking on each other, nothing more, as he's very loyal and I respected his marriage. While scrolling through Facebook in April 2011 I saw his status about the passing of his wife. Let me be honest, I was happy as I thought to myself I can finally have him but then sadness overtook me as I knew exactly how he was feeling - lost, broken and as if his world was over, as I had experienced similar on the passing of my mother four years before from the same dreaded disease - Cancer.

When the funeral was over, and he was trying to put his life back he reached out to me as he was inviting both me and my brother (his best mate) to a memorial for his deceased wife in the morning and a celebratory birthday party in the evening for his mum and stepdad as he was returning to Trinidad and Tobago for vacation.

Well of course I didn't attend the memorial, (no brainier there), although I did make plans to attend the evening do, but of course it was being held in deep West and I was in the East and at that point I didn't have a personal vehicle, so I decided against going in the end.

I was at home with my niece and her friends, as my niece was living with me at the time. While chilling with them she asked me; "Aunty, I thought you were going out with Uncle Rene?" I replied, "I don't have any means of getting to Chagaramas". Then I had a light bulb moment, 'I wonder who the dispatcher of transport was at one of the departments' in my then company.

Off I went to make a call, and lo and behold it was a person who I used to talk to. All I can say is that kindness goes a long way and he said that he would send a driver for me. Oh, my days! My heart was pounding, my palms got sweaty - I am going to meet the love of my life.

All dressed and ready to go, the driver arrived to take me on my journey. My mind was racing "what was I going to say?", "how should I react?" It's been five years since I was saw him! I last saw him with his deceased wife in 2006 and my heart broke. I literally ran away in tears leaving them with my mum and brother talking.

Nervously entering the building, I saw him in the distance. My stomach was in knots, my heart was feeling as if it was about to burst out of my chest! Have you ever felt like that?

I was walking towards him, he turned around and smiled at me. I just melted, seeing him in the flesh was the most bewildering experience.

Summer 2011 was lifechanging for me. We were inseparable. He accepted my three children as his own, which made my heart full of joy. All a single parent wants, is for their partner to accept and love their children.

August 2011 came. The dreaded month that our fairy-tale was coming to an end as he had to return to England as school was opening for his daughters. The day of his departure we both cried our eyes out at the airport. I was sad and, in my mind, I was thinking that it was the END. He was going back to his life in the UK and at this point I wasn't sure if he held any interest for anyone else in England, so we said our goodbyes.

It felt like a daze. I cried from the time I left the airport to the time I got home, and I cried myself to sleep that night. I woke up the next morning, still broken from the day before, but I also felt that I had to get back to reality for my children's sake, so I got on my knees and started to pray; "Dear God, I pray for someone to love me for me and to love my three children as his". Then, suddenly, my phone rang at exactly 9:15am. It was him!

God had answered my prayers. He had called to say that they had arrived safely and when he gets home, he'll call me once he settles. Now I was excited!! I felt as if my world was now complete. I finally had the man I've loved since my teens.

I waited patiently - kept looking at my mobile. After three hours of waiting, he called. There were the butterflies in my stomach again! My heart raced. I answered the call and we spent almost two hours on the phone. I told him that he should go and get some rest because there is a time difference and England was 5hrs ahead in time, so my day was now starting, and he was in the middle of his. I knew he was very tired, so he needed his rest as he had just been travelling and also had his two young daughters to deal with, and trust me, I know that you need all the energy for that.

Our relationship developed by late night Skype calls, telephone calls and WhatsApp messages. In November 2011 for my birthday, my son and I flew to London for a week to celebrate it with him and his daughters. It was magical and amazing! It did break my heart to leave my girls behind, but they had school, so I had no other choice. It was time for their dad to step up.

That was the most beautiful birthday I had ever celebrated in my thirty-seven years of my life. I spent it with my soulmate, my destiny, my everything. I left London after the week, feeling as if I was on top of the world. My heart was filled with love and joy, and I couldn't wait to see him again.

I flew home and went back to work, when I was talking to a colleague about my experience, (someone I looked up to as a mother figure). She turned to me and said that I shouldn't be putting my life on hold because I wasn't sure what he was doing in London, but no man would want me as I've got three children! I was taken aback, shocked and upset by her words.

Boy was she wrong!! Christmas 2011 and I was back in London with my three children and my niece, (I couldn't leave her at home as she was living with me and so she was classed as my fourth child). We had the most magical time that Christmas. My daughters enjoyed their vacation thoroughly and I was finally happy.

I returned to Trinidad and Tobago in January 2012, with a rock on my finger.

"Oh my God I was engaged to him!" How exciting.

I remember telling him that he didn't propose. His reply was that he didn't have to as it was already written by God and so we decided that we would get married in the U.K.

So, on Sunday 29th January 2012, I left for the U.K. as we made the appointment with the registry office in the local borough. We got legal advice also and were advised that I had to contact my local High Commission for legalities. As soon as I returned after Easter, I would make that appointment. But for now, it was time to enjoy our time together as best as we could.

Yes, I was missing my daughters as this was the longest that we've been apart and with that, I started to literally count down their arrival. The night before my daughters were to arrive in the U.K. I couldn't sleep. I was nervous as I just wanted to hold them close and never let them go again. I missed them so much. After Easter, I returned home and called the U.K. High Commission in Trinidad to get the information to submit to them. After that the next step was to have a physical interview with an immigration officer.

About a month later, I received a phone call from the High Commission to say that I had an appointment. At the appointment I started giving our history and how long we've known each other. The officer was in utter shock. He then said to me, "You guys were meant to be together!" YES, WE WERE!

With the interview now completed, the nail biting began. It felt like forever! Whilst waiting I had a bit to occupy my mind, as my eldest was due to take the Secondary Entrance Assessment. She was eleven, so helping her study kept me busy. I also started reading a book called 'The Purpose Driven Life' by Rick Warren and I would read a chapter a day. The insight and knowledge I got from that book was phenomenal, not to mention the strength. I became invincible because I felt like I could take on anything and anyone! It truly was freeing.

Anthony and the girls returned to enjoy another summer holiday in Trinidad, and we made that summer as memorable as we could.

In August I got the phone call! Oh my God! Time to collect my documents!!

I was squealing, butterflies were in my stomach, my heart was racing, my palms were sweating as we all went to collect the documents. Anthony assured me that if it went negatively for us, he was prepared to pack up everything and return to

Trinidad because chances like what we've got don't happen in lifetimes, so he wasn't letting me go.

I took a deep breath. Documents in my hand I took them out with closed eyes as I was incredibly nervous. I opened my eyes and there they were - our Visas were approved. I screamed so loudly, and we both hugged each other crying. The five children were also screaming and crying we were all excited and happy.

Anthony and his daughters were returning to the U.K. on 4th September 2012 so we set the plan in motion for my children and myself to join as quickly as we could. We checked the flights and it said I could leave a week later - 11th September 2012. The reality had sunk in. I was literally packing up my life in suitcases and going to start over in a different country- me and my three children.

I bid farewell to my loving fiancé and his daughters on 4th September 2012 and this goodbye was not as painful because we knew that within a week, we would all be together. Now it was time to pack up approximately sixty-two years of life in four suitcases (that's my thirty-seven, my first born twelve, my second born eleven and my son's two). I knew this mission would be accomplished if I called in my bestie, my right hand, my twin from another mother Nyokha. And so, I am blessed that she helped, and I'll be forever grateful. The best part of migrating for my daughters, was that they would not have to start the new school year in Trinidad, so they got an extended summer vacation.

The day came. "It's here - we are travelling today" I thought. We left for the airport that afternoon with my bestie Nyokha, my daughters' dad, both my daughters' best friends. The whole contingent walked us to the departure gate. We again hugged, cried, and said our goodbyes.

My life in Trinidad and Tobago was over. Time to board the aircraft came and my heart was pounding. We walked down the aisles on the plane and found our seats. We all got comfortable, and I made sure that they all were firmly strapped in. I closed my eyes and imagined my new life while smiling.

On Tuesday 12th September 2012, mine and my children's feet touched U.K. soil. It was so exciting! This was going to be our new home until God decides otherwise. We disembarked, collected our luggage, and walked out to the departure lounge. My future husband and his daughters' waiting for us. I walked towards him and collapsed in his arms in tears. Relief and excitement wrapped up in a hug. It was time to build our future together.

We chose our wedding date of Saturday 15th December 2012. I couldn't think straight over the next couple of weeks as my head was literally spinning. I was giddy with excitement. This felt like a dream. Moving thousands of miles across the ocean and now marrying the love of my life.

We kept our wedding so simple, as this was both our second time doing it, and so I walked up the aisle as Miss Karlene Collins. After an hour, I walked out the building as Mrs Anthony Jordan. The universe had this written for us.

No matter what - never be afraid to take that first step because you never know where it can take you!

DEDICATION

To all single Mums in the world, know that you can always find your happy ever after.

Karlene Jordan

Karlene Jordan is a 46yr old mum of five and is married to her soulmate.

She works for the National Health Service (NHS), and she is also a Professional Network Marketer. She was drawn to network marketing as her son has a type of cerebral palsy called spastic diplegia.

Her passion has and will always be helping others and being kind, as being helpful makes a difference in the world. Her dream is to open a special needs football club for those suffering with any form of spastic cerebral palsy.

WEBLINKS:

Facebook Personal - https://www.facebook.com/karlene.collins
Instagram – https://www.instagram.com/blessedkarlene
Twitter https://mobile.twitter.com/karlenejordan
LinkedIn https://www.linkedin.com/mwlite/in/karlene-jordan

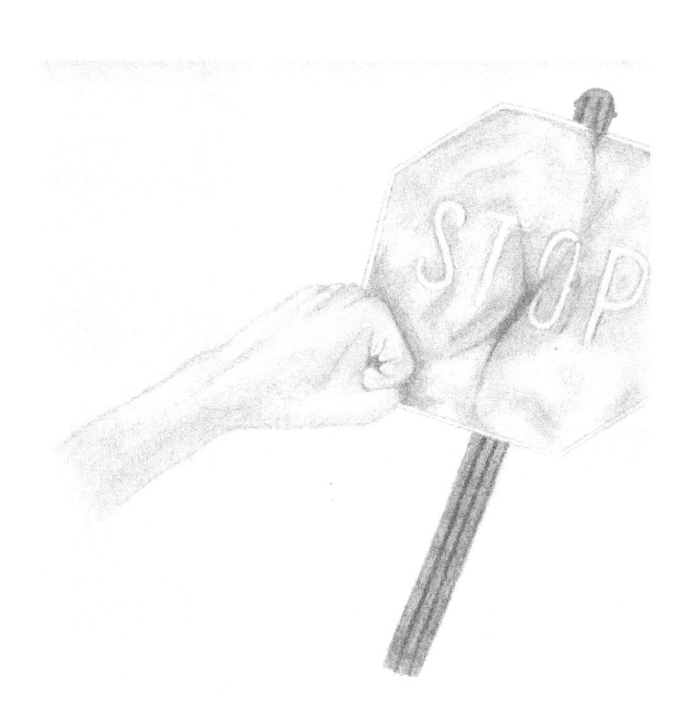

"No matter how bad a situation is, there is always a way out, even if you just have one person to lead you out of that dark situation, that is all you need".

Mandy Vermaak

"Just Hold My Hand – We Will Be Safe"

I wanted to share a part of my life that I haven't shared with others, but strongly believe it can help someone heal their pain in their lives and let them know they not alone.

My story starts when I was very young and as any child, I wanted a happy carefree life. My mom was in the medical profession and even though she worked crazy hours, she was the most amazing mom anyone could wish for. She worked many hours to be able to pay bills and buy what was needed in the home. I was an only child, so there was never a sibling to play with, so my mom made sure she was there within her busy schedule to give me the time and love that I needed.

But there was a part of this life that wasn't so perfect and that's what I want to share with you.

One part that was kept away from outsiders knowing… My dad.

The person that *should* protect you and care for you, was the one that tried to hurt me the most as a child.

We moved into a lovely house in a beautiful town as it was becoming summer. It was the ideal weather to be outside and play. My mom would, on her off days from the hospital, sit outside while I would do what most young children do - climb trees, swing, and make mud pies.

But of course, when it was time to go inside, there would be a secret fear that always waited for us. My father was an alcoholic.

Yes, I know some will say that there are many that are the same, but in my case, my father became very violent when he was drunk. The sad part was that he never just had one drink. He would finish one or two bottles of brandy at once. I remember feeling nervous and scared even though I was very young. Knowing that the slightest thing could trigger an outburst of shouting and screaming and breaking things. I would walk past him and pray that he would just fall asleep.

The other sad part was that, in those days, divorce was never a choice. 'Til death us do part and for better or worse' was the motto.

As many times I'm sure, what happened in homes was kept very quiet.
So, after a day of fun outside, I had my bath and my dinner. Then it was time to get ready for bed. I would go into the bathroom to wash my hands and brush my teeth and then it was time to cuddle with my favourite teddy Benji. "Finally, bedtime" … or so I thought.

Then came the loud talking, the banging of things and the disgusting language. I would hear my mom tell him to keep his voice down and with that, he would shout even louder. "No… not again", I would think to myself. For hours he would carry on and while he was ranting, my mom would come into my room and tell me to hide.

"Go to your hiding place", my mom would say. And without questioning her, I would crawl under my bed, behind my toy boxes. Eventually the noise would stop, and I would feel my mom's gentle hand softly touch my leg, to let me know he had finally passed out and was sleeping.

I knew my mom was scared, but being strong in her own way, she made me feel safe.

So, the night became day and my mom got me ready for school with a packed lunch and juice and we headed for the bus. Even though my mom had a car license, she wasn't able to afford a car. We would quietly leave the house, so not to wake my dad that was still sleeping after all the alcohol the night before.

The routine was that after school, my teacher would make sure I got on the school bus safely and I would then be dropped off at a bus stop near my aunt, where she was waiting. There I would stay till my mom finished work. My aunt would then walk me back to the bus stop and make sure I was on the bus and then I would meet my mom near her work. From there we would walk home together.

At the time I would enjoy running and giggling with my mom, while we walked, not realizing that she must have been exhausted. She always had, what my mom called 'magic sweets or treats' in her handbag, which of course I enjoyed a lot. As we came closer to home you could feel the tension, and it was because we never knew what was waiting for us there.

We opened the door slowly. A sigh of relief, he wasn't there. I placed my school bag down in the front entrance and went with my mom to the kitchen. Supper was started and my mom was picking up the empty alcohol bottles left lying around from the previous night.

Then…. the sound of a gate opening. "No please", I thought. Hoping it was not my dad. But yes, he was home. Still drunk and bumping the side of the gate when driving in. He walked into the house. My mom had finished supper by this time and dished up. We ate in dead silence, not knowing what was going to happen next. He walked back to the car, fetched a paper bag from it and well, we knew what was inside. 3 bottles of brandy again.

"Where did you get money for alcohol?", my mom asked, as he wasn't working. With a smirk on his face he replied, "None of your business", and took a glass and made his way to the living room. My mom ran my bath water and helped me get ready for bed. I had just gotten settled into bed and then… there was the same awful shouting again. Doing as I was told; I went to hide until he had passed out. This carried on night after night, and I guess you can say I thought it was normal.

My mom decided that she wouldn't buy much food for the home, hoping it would force him to make a plan to go to work. So, it was discussed that my aunt would feed me supper just before I took the bus home, and my mom would have something to eat at work. He was furious when there was no food - banging and breaking things. This time causing such a racket that a neighbour came to investigate what was going on, to which my dad then got in the car and left.

Off to school and my mom looking so exhausted, smiled, hugged, and kissed me on the forehead and said everything will be okay.

Days passed and my dad hadn't returned home. In a way I hoped he never would. Then late on a Thursday night we heard him drive in, park, and open the front door. He made his way straight to the living room and fell asleep there. We left the next morning, not even talking to him and hoped when we returned home, he would be sober and in a good mood.

We arrived home. Wait… where was most of our furniture? Have we been robbed? The front door was still locked, no sign of a break-in anywhere. Then a neighbour came over and said he thought we were moving. "Moving? No, we are not moving", my mom said. Well, my dad had only come back home and taken certain items.

My mom was extremely angry and asked the neighbour what time this all happened. My mom and I began to cry as we noticed all my toys, dolls and teddies were gone. Did he really stoop so low to take that too? Well, he had, and he said to the neighbour it was to give to his drinking friends' children.

As days became weeks, and weeks became months, life became pretty much better than normal, and my gran spoke to my mom and told her she needed to file for divorce and that she would pay for it. So, that's exactly what my mom did, and it was placed in motion. My dad was furious and said how dare my mom even think of leaving him. But my mom said 'enough was enough and we deserved a better life'

This was not going to be the end of the fear.

We arrived home one day and not suspecting anything we unlocked the door and entered the house. No!! My dad was there - already drunk. What now?!

My mom, still holding my hand asked him what he was doing there. He was so drunk already, 2 empty bottles on the floor next to him. He was so angry and so aggressive. Swearing at my mom and saying he won't leave the house, he then got up from the chair and before we could do anything he was standing next to me.

He had a .38 Special gun in his hand.

He opened it and said "Look, only one bullet in the barrel". Then lifted the gun and pointed it against my head. Laughing he said," let's see how lucky you are today". Then spun the barrel and pulled the trigger. Click it said.

"Well, well", he laughed "you are lucky" and then he did it over and over again. By now I was numb with fear, but I was not going to show any emotion, as I decided I wasn't focused on what was going on. "That's annoying", he eventually shouted as it didn't fire off a shot. I remember shaking all over from fear and the tears were running down my mom's face. "Stop crying", he shouted and moved to the chair to get another drink.

At that moment my mom grabbed my hand and started walking out the front door. She looked at me and said, "Just don't look back, just keep walking and don't run neither". From the front door he shouted; "come back or I'll kill you both". But my mom kept walking until we were out the front gate.

I remember arching my back wondering when a bullet would hit me, but my mom holding my hand tight in hers, said "Everything will be okay".

What I learned from this moment in my life, is that - no matter how bad a situation is, there is always a way out and when you have even just one person to lead you out of that dark situation, that is all you need and that is when you truly find what the meaning of inner strength means.

DEDICATION

I dedicate my chapter to my beautiful Mom. For your courage, inner strength, and determination you gave me a better life and I am so grateful. You showed me to not settle and that everything will be okay.

Mandy Vermaak

Mandy was born in England, in a small town called Barnett and moved to South Africa with my mom and dad at the age of 2 years old. She was actually named Amanda.

Mandy has 3 amazing children and though they are very different in many ways, they are also very similar in some things they do. They are her true-life joy.

She has many years of banking experience and she always wanted to work with art, but becoming a mom, became her main purpose. Now that her children have grown, she is following some of her passions, they grown, one of which is writing and the other is rediscovering herself.

Mandy has been fortunate to be part of Rebecca Adams' International Interview Series 2020 and she has also assisted an online network marketing coach. Her 'side hustle' is a healthy beverage company and some online trading.

WEBLINKS:

Facebook Wall: https://www.facebook.com/mandy.vermaak

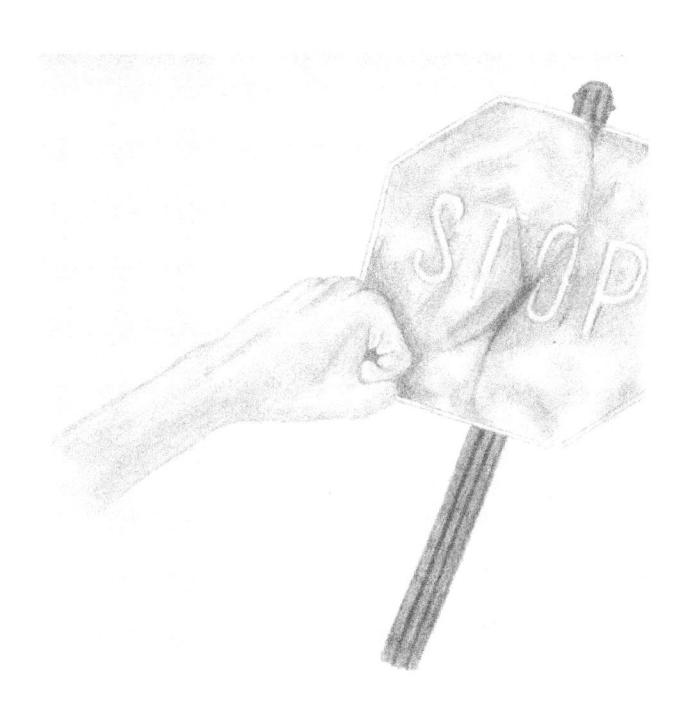

"You get one life, so live, laugh and love your way through it"

Victoria Sainsbury-Brown

Given a Second Chance so Going to Live It!

It was a warm and sunny day in late spring 2011. I had just put the phone down, after my mum told me that my Nan has just been diagnosed with bowel cancer

I was shocked and surprised as we had only been discussing her problems recently and we all had thought that it was her IBS playing up again, as most of the women in my family suffer this, including myself.

My Nan means so much to me. I spent a lot of time with her growing up and she always made me laugh. My heart fell to my stomach at the thought of how sick she was, and I suddenly felt regret… at living further away from my family and never getting to see them all enough. I just wanted to go and hug her and tell her everything would be ok. I felt worried and scared for my Nan, and my mum did not go into too much detail on the phone. She just made me promise to get myself checked out also, as my nan and myself had been having the same kind of symptoms.

I felt sick with worry making the doctor's appointment. Lots of thoughts going around in my head, as you can imagine. Surely my nan and I couldn't both be diagnosed at the same time with the same cancer? I didn't have time to be sick! Being a single parent to an ASD child and working, what would I do? My doctor assured me I was too young for bowel cancer so that put my mind at rest for a while.

Then, over the next few months, my nightmare began… as I slowly got more ill. I kept getting told repeatedly that it was just constipation and not to worry. I couldn't eat and struggled to even drink and was eventually signed off work, which scared me a lot as I had to look after my son and provide for him and I was struggling every day.

It was now December 2011 and after a lot of tests, major weight loss and vomiting so many times a day (I lost count), the most intense pains that I had ever felt, and being dismissed by doctors wherever I went, I finally got a doctor to agree to a CT scan which showed *I did have bowel cancer.*

Questions started to appear in my head of - How could I have bowel cancer? I thought I was too young. Funnily enough I almost felt relieved when I was told. After so long of being told it was nothing and feeling like a fraud, I finally had a reason and understanding of why I was so ill.

I was told over the phone to come straight in to pick up some medication to do overnight, as I had to have more tests the next day. Later that night my bowel had finally had enough and burst!!

I was rushed to hospital to try and save my life. I was so scared and vomiting lots of blood. I had to have an emergency stoma fitted, which meant they could now concentrate on radiotherapy and chemotherapy to shrink my tumour so that they could eventually take it out.

All of this happened whilst my son slept warm and cosy in his bed with my mum looking after him. My poor boy went to sleep with me at home and woke up wondering where I was. He even called my mobile during the night and left a heart-breaking message as he could not find me and wondered where I had gone.

I received this message after being in hospital for around a week and hearing the message was heart wrenching and I cried thinking how scared he must have been. I was so scared for myself through all of this but more scared for him. I was supposed to be there for him and to protect him and now I couldn't. He would, now at eleven years of age, be the one who wants to protect and help look after me.

He was there helping to lift me up and care for me through my treatment. He even came to watch me have my last radiotherapy session, which no child should have to go through - he witnessed so much so young. I remember a conversation with the lady from the hospice team that helped us as he simply asked her if I would die. Being his usual self and wanting to know all the facts which is part of his asd, the lady, not wanting to lie to him, simply said that she was not sure, however all the doctors would do their very best to help make me better and hopefully get me through this.

That broke my heart to sit next to him whilst he was being told this. He was so brave, and I struggled to keep back the tears at the thought of not being with him. He was and still is my whole world.

He grew so much through all of this and pushed himself so much at his first year in senior school as he put all of his effort, frustration and worry into his learning. It was such a horrendous journey to go on, however I was still so concerned about my Nan. They had managed to remove her cancer quickly and she seemed to be on the mend.

It was now July 2012 and the day I was finally getting rid of the tumour; it had shrunk enough to come out, plus I had to have a full rapid hysterectomy. It was the same day that my nan was taken into a hospice, as her cancer had returned, and she was now terminal.

In August, whilst I was concentrating on healing, my nan passed away. I struggled so much with this news because I wished I could have been there for her. It left me with lot of questions, including "why her? and not me? why did I survive?". I struggled with my nan's illness and death for a long time and finally went to counselling, which helped a lot, as today, I am able to talk about her again without breaking down so much.

I have been left with a lot of long-term conditions, which we believe could have been caused by the cancer or the treatment and the surgeries I had to have in order to save my life. I am unable to digest food very well, suffer from lymphatic colitis and have fibromyalgia to name a few. I am in pain constantly; fatigued and struggle every time I eat food. I have migraines and a lot more frequently too. I tried to go back to work after around two and half years off, but it did not work out because I could no longer do my job as I once did, and so my doctor advised that I may find it impossible to go back to work and have the same life I once had.

I started suffering from depression and resting in bed most of the time, and with being a single mum to a boy with learning disabilities, made it even harder. His smile and love kept me going, but I did lose the urge to fight for life.

Then in 2016 my doctor told me I will never get better and could stay bedridden if I did not try to start getting out and about and move my body. With the fibro, he warned me that it would be painful but the more I could stay active the better. Sounded like a plan, so I found a dog walking group and got myself an active puppy, as my other two little dogs were not really bothered about walking. I needed a dog that would get me up and going and needed a lot of walks.

So off I went. I started meeting new people for dog walks and slowly walking more and more each day. Now, do not get me wrong, it hurt a lot and I would have to rest all the time after, but slowly, I could walk further and further, and it really started to help my depression too. I started to imagine that I could try and get my life back on track.

Then in 2017, not long after finally being put in full remission - another knock back! My boyfriend of ten years who had helped me so much through all my treatments and illness left me!

I was devastated and heartbroken, which knocked me right back and I struggled to fight on. But then in 2018, a year after, I found out that my sister and my ex were now dating - so a double whammy!!

I kept trying to get back up but life just kept knocking me back down! I was determined to get back out in the world and try and live my life the best I could - whatever life kept throwing at me. It was hard and I needed a lot of support from family to get me back out there.

So, in 2019 when I met my new boyfriend whilst out dog walking with the group, that was great. I didn't expect it, but it felt good to start dating again (it had been a long while). Not long after, in 2020 pre-lockdown, we started talking about how I could get out and manage to work again. I really wanted to get back out there and thought that it may also help my depression and my fitness levels, whilst getting my brain active again. However, it would be hard. I would need a very understanding boss who could understand my illnesses, fatigue and that I was not able to stand or sit for too long.

I have always loved animals and have done some training in the past and would love to work with them again, totally different from being a trained pharmacy dispenser, which was what I was doing when I first became ill.

I had a real interest in raw feeding and herbal medicines, so my boyfriend and I discussed it lots and thought it would be a great idea if we opened a raw shop and

I could be my own boss. All my dreams were coming true. I would love my own business, so even though we were in lockdown and the struggles that came with, we thought "let's do this".

We found a shop and got to work at getting my dream started. It was hard work - physically and mentally but I was loving it. My designs and ideas were coming to life - the name, the logo (all in big letters above the shop door), decorating and designing the shop and how I wanted it to look. Kevin said that it should all be me as it was my dream, so I should be able to do everything the way I wanted it, which was fabulous of him as I could never have started this adventure without his help. I wanted everything natural looking as it was going to be a raw and natural pet supplies shop and considering there is not another raw shop where I live, I wanted it to be fabulous.

I got shelving with natural baskets made, nice chunky wood shelves and picked my colour scheme of grey and pink. It was slowly coming together, but the long days of sorting everything out, finding suppliers etc were taking a toll on my body. I was more sore and very tired, however, I kept on pushing through as it was making me so happy and made me feel like I had a purpose again. All the studying into raw feeding was finally going to become something. I got to hire my first employee who happened to be my friend Hazel. She also loved animals and knew about my health issues, she could understand me and what I was going through, no questions asked, if I ever needed to rest and she knew my limitations.

It was not long, and we were ready to open, I was finally back at work after nine years of illness and fighting back to be healthy.

The shop is going so well that after only ten months we are looking for new properties to open another shop to help keep up with the demand. It is going from strength to strength, and I am loving every day.
I am busy, fatigued and still sore every day. Some days the pain gets so bad that I want to go back to hiding in my bed and cry just like the old days, but you know

what! No more....

Through my mental and physical scars, heartbreak, depression, betrayal, and pain - I am finally happy.

The doctors said I may never work again, and I know I will always struggle; however, I hold my head up high knowing whatever happens in life and tries to knock me down, I am alive. I am a fighter and a survivor.

I have my fabulous son and my family who have always been there to support me. My boyfriend who has helped me so much and my gorgeous three dogs who keep me going every day. After all I have been through, I am very thankful to still be here and all that I have, I always try to live by my favourite mantra live, love laugh....

"Live everyday like it is your last, love with all your heart and laugh loudly and often".

DEDICATION

I dedicate this chapter to my wonderful son Harrison. You are my world and I thank you for being strong and always by my side. Whatever we face in life, we can do it together as a team x

Also, to my mum and dad for both being there and helping me through the worst time of my life, and guiding and encouraging me through my challenges and dreams x

Victoria Sainsbury-Brown

Victoria is a proud single mum to her son Harrison, who has special needs, and is a mum to her three fur babies Lola, Rosie and Peppa. She loves spending time out walking, camping with family and just being at home with her son and dogs relaxing.

She grew up in Hanworth, Middlesex near Heathrow Airport. She has lived in Dorset and then moved to Swindon, Wiltshire in 2007, to start a new life as a single parent where she still resides.

Victoria has experience in sales and customer service. She was a trained pharmacy dispenser and is now the proud owner of the only Raw and Natural pet supplies shop in Swindon, which is going fabulous and growing daily.

She loves her job and gets to meet amazing people and their dogs too as she loves to help all the dogs daily.

Through telling her story, in this book, she would like to help make sure that no one else gets told that they are too young to get this disease and to fight for a diagnosis. To show that with strength, determination and a lot of love and support with whatever life battles you are faced, you can come through the other side.

WEBLINKS:

Personal Facebook
https://www.facebook.com/victoria.sainsburybrown
Instagram https://www.instagram.com/victoriasainsburybrown
Facebook Page: https://www.facebook.com/Raw4Pawz-Swindon-111808397250838/
Instagram: https://www.instagram.com/raw4pawzlimited
Website: https://www.raw4pawz-swindon.co.uk/
Email: raw4pawz-shop@raw4pawz-swindon.co.uk

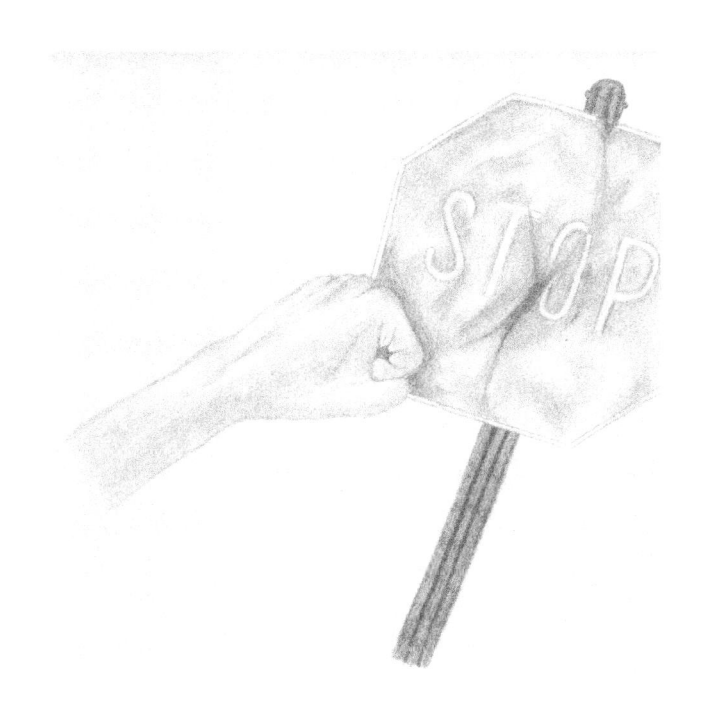

"With God and a positive attitude, you really can make it through everything".

Sherri Olsen

To Tell You my Story is to Tell of Him!

I had been working out for a while to get ready to go from a stationary bike, of many years, to a real bike outside and I'd moved within a mile of my office so I decided I could start riding my bike to and from work but……

I didn't realize that I should have practiced before I got onto the bike because it was a large bike and very different to what I was used to.

The first day I got to work and boy, I thought I was really cool! Sweat was dripping down my face as I had my helmet on. I told my co-workers that I was a real biker chick now! It felt good and I was so happy.

The second day I decided to go in a different direction to work and I got to our Main Street and suddenly, my bike tires hit the new tar and gravel prior to the crossing. In that moment my bike flipped up into the air, upside down and I went kerplunk down on the ground.

A real life 'Superman' came running towards me and made sure I was safe. He called the ambulance, and I was rushed to the hospital. The ambulance drivers I had on that ride were amazing! What a whirlwind!

After they got me sedated, I was telling them I loved them, and they were like "you mean brotherly Love, right?" and I said, "well of course brotherly Love", but half of them ended up staying up there at the hospital to make sure I was okay because apparently, we formed a little bond.

The x-rays revealed that I had shattered my hip and broke my femur at the top, all the way through. Wow! So, what they proposed to do was put a titanium rod through my upper left thigh buttocks area down to my knee and then screw it in at the knee midway, and also put a big screw in to put the hip socket back into place.

At the time they didn't tell me that I only had a 20% chance of living!!

The internal bleeding and damage was quite extensive and I was 59 years old but thankfully I was in great physical condition.

I had the elder associates from my church who came and gave me a priesthood blessing and I was filled with peace. They said the surgery went really well and I, myself, felt like I was doing really well too, but on day 4, I came to, and my ER nurse John was sitting there. I said, "what are you doing back up here?". His reply shocked me. He said, "we're losing you and we don't know what to do"!!

I said, "well that's okay I'm clean and pure and ready to go". His reply was, "that's really good you feel that way considering the predicament you are now in. Do you want to be resuscitated or not?". I answered, "oh no don't resuscitate me, just let me go".

At the time I was feeling Heavenly Bliss and so much peace, Love, and joy. John said, "okay will you sign your 'No Resuscitate Order?" I said yes and signed it. Just then I heard that the elders were in the hospital and if anyone needed a blessing then they would come and do one, so I asked them for a blessing.

They came into my room and anointed my head with oil and laid their hands upon my head. I remember it was a beautiful blessing of health and healing but the only thing I recall them saying, while I had my eyes shut and I saw Jesus in my mind waving his finger at me, was "Your Heavenly Father wants you to know He is not done with you yet".

Within an hour I was sitting up in bed - all my vitals were normal, and my room was filled with doctors and nurses saying, "oh my goodness we have never seen anything like this before, what just happened?". All I could say was "Jesus happened" and they said "obviously", because there was no medical explanation.

The next day my doctor came in to see me in the morning, scratching his head as the on-call doctor had just been communicating with him what had happened with me. I asked him what was wrong, and he said, "I've been scratching my head all night over you. At first, I was losing you and then suddenly you're just fine. It's amazing!".

I explained that the elders came to see me, gave me a blessing, and said that the Heavenly Father wasn't done with me yet. He threw his head back and his hand went over his head as he said, "Sometimes in life there are things that happen that there is just no medical explanation for" - in other words a full-blown miracle. That was me!

The very next day I was transported to the nursing home 30 miles away. The doctor and therapist told me that when I left the hospital eventually, I'd have to move out of my loft apartment that I had just leased from my boss, because I could never do stairs again.

167

The nursing home therapist told me the same thing, so my daughter and my friend proceeded to pack up my place. I asked my boss to please help me find something that was one level to live in. Unfortunately, he replied telling me that there was absolutely nothing at all available as the college students had all come back and that I'd have to crawl up the stairs! Shocked!

I went to physical therapy and started practicing stairs. It was tough and testing but within three weeks I was up to 50 stairs. By the time I got home, (three and a half weeks later), I only had to master the 18 steps to my door. It was still challenging to walk up but I had a cane, and I had a walker and railings to help me. I grabbed them and held on. I was determined to show people and myself that I could do it.

I did it! I made it!

I had to stay at home for a full 30 days without leaving. My home healthcare team came to teach me how to walk again and a week later I was able to pull myself up the stairs at the office and I continue to go up and down the stairs ever since that day.

On some days I was up to 11 flights of stairs and at the 20-month mark - I realized that I could run up and down the stairs. So, I set out to climb the mountain I had my eye on. I was able to do it and make it to the top of the wind caves in our Canyon! What a truly glorious accomplishment. Words can't even describe!

God truly is a god of Miracles and to tell you my story is to tell of Him. I'm doing better and better every day and sometimes I say in every way.

<u>Some of the things that I have learned from this experience I wanted to share with you as a go-to guide. Take note of these in a journal and read them.</u>

You never know for sure what day you will leave this Earth, so have things in order.

Always take time in life to appreciate your life, health, and all your amazing daily blessings, as you stay in the present moment. Focus on gratitude and take one day at a time, as you will be able to have an exceptional life.

Always put God first. He is number one and realize how much He Loves you and you mean so much to Him.

Stay positive and as soon as the negative thought enters your brain, cast it out and replace it with a positive. We are programmable beings and what we think about, we bring about and what we focus on expands, so the more positive you are, the more positive your life will be or vice versa - there is no other way.

We are here on Earth to help bring Heaven to Earth. Our deeds and actions are noted always as we are basically students at the Earth Academy where we have the most amazing Virtual Technology and real-life simulations. Life is our oyster, and we are the beautiful and rare pearls which are of great worth in the sight of God, just as other stones, like the diamond, must be chiselled through and go through some rough spots to become the most beautiful that it possibly could be.

Know that when we look at our lives from a different perspective, we can see that we personally grow and we are the captains of our vessels and so, it's up to us to sail across all the obstacles as smoothly as possible and find joy in our journey. It was created for us all to have joy, but we are the ones who must do the work.

At times we will get thrown off course, but we can continue to reach our end goals, which for the most, is a life of peace, Love, joy, and happiness.

Never give up, even though the going gets tough. God created some strong warriors and when you see a Goliath in front of you, remember that's because God knows you have a David inside of you and that you're also human royalty (Children of the Divine).

Rest if you must and always take great care of yourself. Love yourself - as you would the person that you love most in the world by lovingly pampering yourself. Eat well, exercise and enjoy the finer things in life. Surround yourself with people who ignite your soul and help you to be excited about life. Stay in the present moment and focus on gratitude.

Believe in yourself, claim your power, rise up and shine.
Remember it's "All Bout Love"

DEDICATION

Dedicated to my Lord and Savior Jesus Christ

Sherri Olsen

Sherri is a realtor and has been for 22yrs. She has a passion for helping sellers and buyers in Commercial, Residential and Agricultural Estate.

She has 14yrs in customer service experience. She is a Lightworker, Reiki Practitioner and has certificates as a CNA certified nurse's aid, communications, travel training and airport reservationist.

Sherri was born in Idaho and moved to Utah when she was 1yrs old. She has 6 children, and a massive family including 17 grandchildren.

She loves to read, go to the mountains, beaches, and parks, mediate and swim.

WEBLINKS:

https://www.facebook.com/sherri.olsen.714

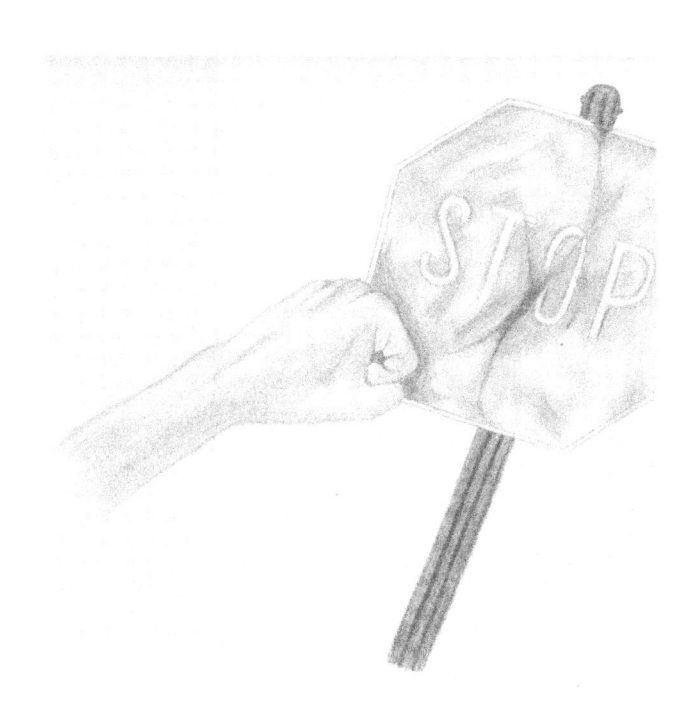

"Would you want your son or daughter in this type of relationship? If not, help them to leave".

Louise Adair

Married to the Wrong One!

When I met him, I remember thinking he was the most amazing person ever.

He came into my life when I was at my lowest. I was self-harming, overdosing, taking numerous drugs, drinking excessively, had severe mental health issues, and I was also struggling with an eating disorder that resurfaced after losing my best friend to suicide a few years before.

If I am honest, I was vulnerable, and he was saying all the right things and convinced me he could give me the life I had always wanted. Within the first week of meeting him in person, I was living with him, and by the end of the first month we were engaged. I know, fast right?!

I did not think that just 5 years later I would be dealing with a break-up that came out of the blue! It is strange, at the time he ended our relationship and marriage, I thought my life was over BUT now, after nearly 2 months later - I have taken my life back and I am loving having my independence again and being free from someone who tried to destroy me.

It is strange to write those words because when I was with him, I never saw him for who he was. After two recent psychiatric hospital admissions and speaking to nurses, doctors, health care assistants, friends, and family, I now realise how bad things were and how much my friends and family were concerned for my wellbeing.

I thought that being married was meant to be like that. That relationships do struggle and especially during the current pandemic that is happening in the world. I also thought that I could not cope without him. Have you ever felt like that? Can you relate? That you couldn't be without the person you're with?

I think I have proved to myself and any haters that I can achieve anything I want. I am a fighter and have been from the moment I was born. I look back on those five years and ask myself, "Why did I stay? Why did I let him treat me that way?" but I know now, I will not put up with that type of relationship again. The red flags were there but I didn't see them at all.

Unwillingly he has shown me that I am strong. I am my mothers' daughter, and I will not let him destroy me. If you are in this type of relationship, you can leave. You do not need to be controlled or made to feel worthless. You can be your own hero and you can overcome every challenge you face. I know as you read this you might think you can fix him, (I thought that too), but in the end, you can't fix someone who wants to control you, manipulate you, gaslight you and make you feel like everything is your fault. I tried for 2 years to fix him, and in the end he nearly won.

When we first broke up, I tried to take my own life two times, and at one point if my best friend had not have read between the lines of my text and realised something was wrong, I would not be writing this. She saved my life that day, she knew something was wrong and managed to get me the support and help that I needed. I will always be grateful for her on picking up on the signs.

During the first 18 months of our relationship, and through our engagement he was amazing, constantly praising me and telling me I was amazing, beautiful and could achieve anything I wanted in life. The day we got married he completely changed, and I now look back at the photos taken on our wedding day and I can see I was blissfully happy, but he looked dead behind the eyes and looked like he regretted the decision. I had never noticed that before, and even now it hurts to think that maybe I was brainwashed and couldn't see how unhappy he was.

I don't regret marrying him as it was the happiest day of my life and it was the only day in my whole life where I felt truly beautiful, but I do regret staying in a relationship where I spent the majority of the last 3 years crying and begging for him to give me attention and affection. I know that I was very dependent on him, as he had isolated me from my friends and tried to isolate me further, but I started to realise that if I lost my friends then he would have complete control. I remember every time we were out for a drive, he would either make fun of me and say he was joking, or he would call me fat and tell me I needed to lose weight. Then he would make comments like, "I preferred you when you were skinny as you looked better and had more confidence".

So, I would then decide that I needed to lose weight to keep him, but any time I made any attempts to lose weight, he would go to a fast-food restaurant and get me a breakfast as he knew I loved that particular fast-food place. However, when I would try to protest and say I was trying to lose weight he would say "if you are that fussed you can have a salad"! Anyone who goes to the fast-food restaurants knows that a salad is not on their breakfast menu. I would then say to him that they don't do a salad at breakfast time, and he would then say, "well then you can just go without". Obviously with him being my husband I had told him everything about my childhood, my teenage years, and my early twenties and about my eating disorder coming back after I lost Heather to suicide. He seemed to get some weird kick out of the fact I struggled with my self-confidence and that I hated how much weight I had gained due to medication for my mental health.

It is strange to think about what I let him get away with. I have since learned that narcissists are extremely charming and have a way of making everyone fall in love with them. I have some friends who still tell me that they did not see this coming. I have also had people ask me, "What did you do?".

I am keeping those people at arm's length, and I am hoping that if they read this chapter, they will realise I did everything I could to save my marriage. I think deep down I knew our marriage was failing but I did not want to admit it. On my wedding day I woke my maid of honour at 5am, telling her I did not want to go through with the wedding. Now I wonder if that was my intuition. Did I know that he was not right for me? I remember feeling extremely nervous and anxious through most of our relationship, to the point I was on so many sedatives. I struggled with severe panic attacks and regular PTSD nightmares. No matter how many tablets I was on, nothing would totally calm me. I was on the maximum of a lot of my medication for my mental health and I feel it was because I knew he was not the guy I thought he was.

I have now been in England just over a month, as I write this, and I am hardly needing any medication now. I am on the bare minimum, and the medical advisors are so pleased. I do have a few nights where I have struggled to sleep but when I lived in Scotland those few nights were most nights. I just could not switch off and I feared my own shadow. So, I am pleased I am improving my sleeping pattern too. I always wake up feeling rested and even though I do still have nightmares, they aren't at the severity they were, which is great news. Until I start psychotherapy and talk things through everything, those nightmares are not going to go away totally but I am able to cope a lot better with them now as well. I no longer fear the unknown.

I am quite happy to get on a bus and travel wherever I need to go and as long as I have my headphones, then traveling doesn't faze me anymore. This is the first time in many years where I can say I am looking forward to my future. I know that one thing is for sure, I never want to be in a relationship that makes me feel worthless, unworthy or makes me hate myself. I did move 290 miles to start afresh and normally that would unsettle me a lot and I would usually end up as a psychiatric inpatient for a few weeks to a few months to try and get me settled.

My mental health has not been perfect, but I am feeling a lot more like the old me. I have not gone back to my old habits of drug abuse, alcohol abuse, self-harm or overdosing which is an amazing improvement for me. I feel like even though the relationship was not perfect, that imperfect relationship taught me a lot about the inner strength that I have. The strength that the women in my family have all had.

I am immensely proud to say that even though my nanny passed away in December 2017, I can feel her presence and know the strength I feel is from my nanny. My nanny was one of the fiercest and most loving women in my life. She taught me that no matter what you face, you do not cower in the corner, you stand up with your fists in front of you, and you defend your values and your morals. You stick up for what you know is right. She would be proud of me, I think.

I knew after an incident in 2019 that I should have walked away from my marriage. I was told by friends and family at that point that I should not put up with him and his behaviour towards me, but I was worried if I walked away, it would look bad on me. With previous relationships I normally walk away as I get scared and I thought that with my marriage I wanted it to work, I did not want to be a divorcee at 33. What would people think?

I would have done anything he asked, and I did do things that did not align with my life purpose. I wonder if that is why I was always so anxious and stressed? He kept telling me I needed to do something with my life, and I did try a few jobs, but I found it hard, working with my anxiety as it wasn't well controlled. I do have a good work ethic but once I start getting overwhelmed, I find myself spiralling into depression and then I end up making myself ill as I get incredibly stressed and my way of coping with that is to ignore the world, stay in bed and pretend I don't exist, which is not something you can do when you are employed.

If I have learned anything from the last 5 years, it is that no matter how much you love someone if they don't want to be with you, or don't want to change - there is nothing you can do. I think if I am to be honest with you, I wanted more than he ever did. I feel like I was so naïve to think he wanted 'forever' with me. As a lot of people have told me, I was vulnerable, and he saw that and knew he had me right where he wanted me. I remember on our last day out together, I jokingly asked if we were to break up what would you say about me and he said he would tell people that I was toxic, controlling, and crazy. Strangely enough even now just over two months later, those are the words that haunt my nightmares, that make the negative thoughts difficult to overcome and regularly make me doubt my sanity.

When I look back, I know that I was honest with him from day one. I told him everything and considering he met me in a mental health support group, and I was in the state I was, I did not expect him to say, during one of our last conversations before I moved, that he didn't know my mental health was that bad. I am eternally grateful for my friends and family who stuck by me through those dark days and who are still rooting for me. Those friendships and relationships are necessary. I feel like I would never have left, even though at the end, it was something I thought about on a regular basis. I didn't want to be the person to give up.

I have come so far, and I have worked so hard to overcome issues that have plagued me from an incredibly young age, but at the end of the day I feel like no matter what I did it would not have been good enough for him. Some days I still cry about my marriage ending, and everything that happened during those five years. I am told that it's okay to cry as it's part of the process, so I am allowing myself to do that. I think the hardest part is that he walked away without any thought or care of how it would affect me. He has tried to contact me a few times but not to ask how I am, but to talk about money! Not once has he asked me how I am. To me that shows exactly how he felt about me.

The Monday after we broke up, I sat and typed him a 5-page, 2000-word letter, and then I asked him if he wanted to read it. He said yes but never even bothered to reply, or acknowledge the hurt that he caused.

My advice to anyone reading this who is in a similar situation, think about whether you would want that type of relationship for your daughter or son. Would you let them go through what you are experiencing right now? If the answer is no, please reach out to me and I can help you set up an escape plan and help you with any emotional support you might need!

DEDICATION

I dedicate this chapter to my dearest Pamela.
No matter what I have done in my life, you have always been my pillar of strength. You inspire me every day. I want to be the best version of myself because I have seen what you have achieved. Thank you for everything. I am incredibly grateful that you came into my life.
Love you forever.

Louise Adair

After taking part in the first book of this amazing trilogy series, written under her married name, Louise felt the pull to take part in this final book.

Louise has always loved to write and started from an incredibly young age writing stories and letters. She loves to crochet and make blankets for her friends and family who are pregnant or going through a tough time. Crocheting gives her the same sense of peace that writing does.

She loves all things Disney and loves nothing more than to get lost in a good book. Her favourite types of books are fictional books about the war time, nurses in the war and books that talk about people overcoming challenges. Louise is also a mental health advocate and wants to campaign and support the minority of people that mental health services say are too complicated to treat. She was once also labelled as complicated and difficult, so she understands the stigma and wants to work alongside the charities and NHS to help change the way people are treated.

She believes everyone should get the same treatment, as she has experienced with her own mental health and her friend's mental health, that a lot of mental health professionals still have a stigmatized view of patients who struggle with personality disorders.

WEBLINKS:

Instagram – https://www.instagram.com/lifewithborderline87
Facebook Wall – https://www.facebook.com/louiseadair1987
Facebook Page – https://www.facebook.com/louiseisanauthor
Email – louisetheauthor2020@outlook.com

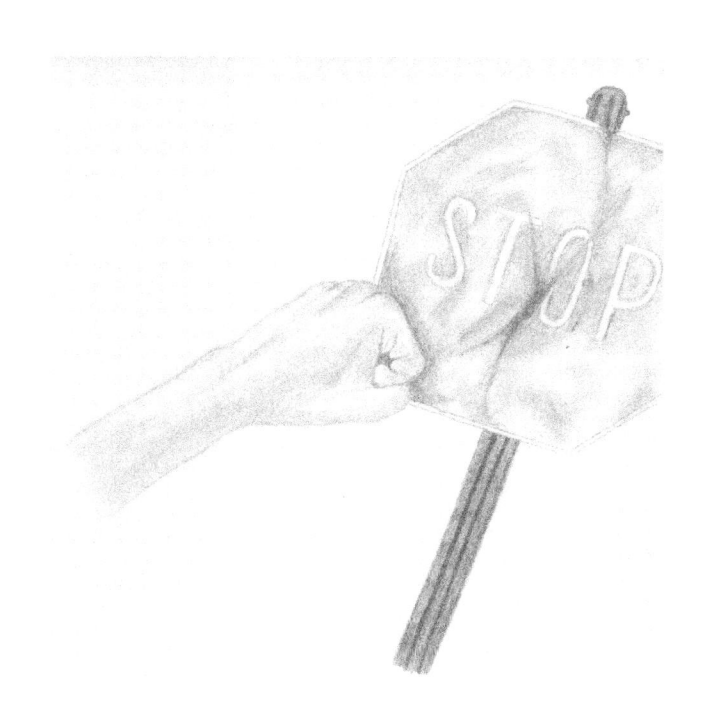

"To me, family is everything. I'll try my best in whatever way I can, even if that means pausing my own life"

Michelle Netherton

The Phone Call I had been Dreading!

To me family is everything, and my heart hurts if anyone is hurt or poorly and I will try my best to help in whatever way I can - even if that means pausing my own life.

I had such a fantastic bond with my big sister Alex. She was always there for me and was even there when my first son was born. Alex was always the joker. In any bad situation, she would be the one making jokes and trying to cheer people up. She always had a twinkle in her eye, and you'd wonder what she was going to get up to next.

It was January 2014 when I tried phoning Alex and I couldn't get an answer. She was living in Devon at the time, and I was down in Cornwall. It felt strange and I had goosebumps forming because I felt like something was wrong. So, I phoned my mum and asked her if she'd heard from Alex, to which she said no. Frantically

I kept phoning and after what felt like hours, Alex answered the phone. She sounded disorientated and was talking really strangely and kept going really quiet…… then the phone went dead.

I immediately called my mum and said there's something wrong with Alex. So, my mum got straight into her car and started driving from Cornwall to Devon, whilst I stayed at home and kept trying to get hold of Alex on the phone.

Mum got to Alex's flat but couldn't get in and at that point I still hadn't managed to get hold of her on the phone either. In that moment, I decided I was just going to call the emergency services. I told them the situation and they got to Alex's place within minutes and broke down the door to find my sister laid on the floor, unable to get up. She was dehydrated and was taken straight to the hospital.

The doctors treated her for dehydration and after a couple of days, Alex was back to her cheeky self, and we discovered that she had been laid on her flat floor for several days after she had a bad reaction to treatment she had had for her hypothyroidism. I really wasn't convinced that this was the only cause and badgered the doctors to do further tests. So, they took bloods and did an MRI.

This is when they found a huge mass in her brain and my sister was diagnosed with Oligodendroglioma (long one isn't it? It's basically a cancerous tumour in the brain).

My heart shattered into a thousand pieces.

'What next?' is what we asked the doctors. They explained that the tumour was so large that it covered the whole frontal lobe of Alex's brain. There were a couple of options that Alex could choose from. One of the options was that they could operate but would only be able to take out half of it because of the positioning. She could then have chemotherapy to try and shrink the remaining half. Alex chose this option but even with the operation, the prognosis was she would only be with us for 18 months after this.

I can't even explain what was going on in my head.

So shortly after this conversation with the oncologist, Alex went into surgery to have half of the tumour removed which she decided to call "Neil". Those hours that she was in the operating theatre, it felt like everything stopped. I was pacing my house waiting for the phone call to say she was out of theatre and okay.

A minute seemed like an hour, but the call finally came. I could breathe.

Once Alex was well enough, she went to our mum's house to recuperate and to start her chemotherapy. Alex didn't last very long with the chemo and decided she didn't want to spend what time she had left feeling ill. I'm sure that was a tough decision to make but we stood by her choice and tried to make things as normal as possible.

We managed to get Alex moved into a flat in Cornwall so she could be close to her family. Alex settled in and started planning things that she wanted to experience, which was good. It was steadily approaching our mum's 60th birthday and Alex decided that she wanted to take her to Africa on safari as our mum loved elephants.

Once they came back, Alex started going on day trips with our brother. Camera in hand they explored lots of waterfalls and she was making memories with him. Alex got a dog to keep her company and to keep her body active and moving. She called him Mika. He was a chocolate Labrador. Alex did so well for a long time and surpassed the doctors estimate of 18 months.

5 years later, is when things started to happen. Alex became really clumsy, and kept falling over a lot and then, out of what felt like nowhere, she started to have seizures. The doctors diagnosed her with epilepsy and started her on medication to try and control them. It was a long process and lots of changing of medication but finally after a couple of months it seemed like we had the right dosage and Alex started back on her mission to experience as much as she could.

We had a good couple of months. She was out a lot taking Mika on walks, visiting our mum, going out with our brother, and spending time with me and my family. Then the seizures started creeping in again. After a particularly bad seizure, we decided it would be a good idea to get Alex an alarm system that would call one of us at the touch of a button if she needed us.

Because of where Alex lived, I would walk past her flat every morning on our school run, so it became a habit to knock on her window and check if she was ok and ask her if she needed anything or she would simply just wave out the window.

One day, however, she wasn't at the window. So, I went up to the window and knocked and got no reply - just a bark from Mika. A shiver went through me. I phoned her mobile phone. Nothing…

That's when panic set in.

Her window was slightly open so I pulled it ajar, and it only opened a little more, but I could reach my hand in and moved the net curtain. All I could see was Alex slumped on the floor, so I quickly closed the net curtain. At that moment I was thankful that at the same time my friend Catherine was walking her daughter to school. I quickly shouted; "Can you take my lot to school?", and she said of course she could.

So, with my children safe, I worked on what to do next. I managed to get a response from Alex, although only a grunt. I threw my hand up the side of the window and tried to reach the safety catch, which opened the window wider, and just managed to get it. YES! I climbed in through the window and checked Alex for injuries. She had a huge gash on the back of her head. I called for the emergency services and with the ambulance on the way, I called my mum.

Alex was taken to hospital and had her head wound treated. She ended up having to stay in hospital for 3 weeks because her seizures just kept coming so badly. She then had to have rehabilitation to help her walk again. This is when it was decided that she needed home help. Alex was not happy about that at all as she was so independent.

After that hospital admission, things started to get bad very quickly. Mum and I were there with her most of each day, taking shifts to take Mika for walks or to make Alex meals because she couldn't stand for very long or walk very far. Shortly after this, Alex decided it wasn't fair to keep Mika any longer, so we rehomed him. It broke all our hearts because he was such a lovely dog. But it was what was needed, and it was best for Mika.

Alex's seizures and falls continued to get worse and by November 2019 she was completely bedridden. I knew then that she was starting to give up. Her sparkle wasn't there as much as before, and she got angry a lot because she couldn't do things for herself. We had carers coming in 4 times a day to help with her personal care and mum and I would sort her meals out between us.

One night I was just getting ready to go to bed when I had a phone call - it was Alex's carer. They had arrived to sort her bedtime out to find her having a seizure, so the emergency services were called. I quickly shoved a hoodie and shoes on and ran to Alex's flat, let myself in and grabbed Alex's rescue medication which is supposed to stop the seizure. It didn't work. Panic set in! "It has to work!"

The second lot of medication didn't work either! One of the carers was still on the phone with the ambulance. They were close and we were telling them that the rescue meds weren't working. The paramedics took over when they arrived but even they couldn't get her seizure completely under control, so it was another trip to the hospital.

Four days later and Alex still hadn't come around from her seizure and we were all called in and told that she was still having a lot of seizures and they were only just managing to keep them under control. They were worried that if she had another grand mal seizure that they might not be able to stop it, and we were then told to prepare for the worst. My mum, brother and I spent the whole day at the hospital with Alex with there was no change.

The next day there were signs that Alex was coming out of it and a week later she was sat up in bed, being cheeky to the nurses once again. Alex was in hospital for a couple of weeks before being allowed home.

More weeks went by of mum and I caring for Alex between us. Christmas came and went in a blur. Before we knew it, the new year had started, and the pandemic hit. It was nearing the end of March when Alex took a turn for the worst again. Another trip to the hospital but because of the pandemic I wasn't allowed to go with her. Several hours later, an A+E consultant rang me to say they had got Alex's seizures under control, but things still weren't looking good. We then made the decision that it was probably time for Alex to go into a hospice because mum and I were struggling with looking after her, even with carers 4 times a day. I knew that was not what Alex wanted but decided it was for the best because she would have 24-hour care and that's what she needed.

April and May 2020 were a blur of travelling to and from the hospice - only one of us allowed in at a time because of the pandemic. Every time I saw her, I could see that sparkle fade away that bit more, until the 18th of June when the hospice phoned and said that things were getting worse.

Alex had stopped eating and drinking, and they advised that we all needed to see her as soon as possible. So, on the 19th of June - a day I will never forget - mum and I went into the hospice. Alex looked as though she was sleeping. The nurses said she hadn't woken up at all in over 24 hours and that they were keeping her as comfortable as possible. We didn't want to leave that day. I think both myself and mum knew that she wasn't going to be with us much longer.

I went to bed that night emotionally exhausted. All I could see was my sister in that bed. Sleep finally took over and I awoke with a start at 5:50am.

I immediately checked my phone. 2 missed calls and a voicemail asking me to phone the hospice. I took a breath, dialled the number, stated who I was and waited for the ward sister to come onto the phone.

That's when she told me that at 2.55am that morning, my sister had passed away peacefully with one of the nurses by her side.

My whole world shattered.

I thanked the nurse and hung up before making the worst call I've ever made in my life to my mum.

DEDICATION

To my amazing big sister Alex. The world feels so strange without you. I couldn't have asked for a better sister. I love you with all my heart. Until we meet again.

Michelle Netherton

Michelle has diplomas in Autism Awareness, ADHD and Child Psychology. She is a Mum of 4 children (3 of which has Special Educational Needs). She lives in Cornwall, UK.

Michelle prides herself on learning as much as she can about the disabilities her children face and has a Child Care NVQ level 3 and is a qualified Senior Co-ordinator. She is also a bestselling co-author in the 2nd book of this "Smashing Through" series titled - "Smashing Through The Brick Wall".

Her hobbies include going to the cinema, knitting, crocheting, reading, going for long walks and exploring with her children.

WEBLINKS:

Instagram: https://www.instagram.com/netherton83
Facebook Wall: https://www.facebook.com/michelle.luff3

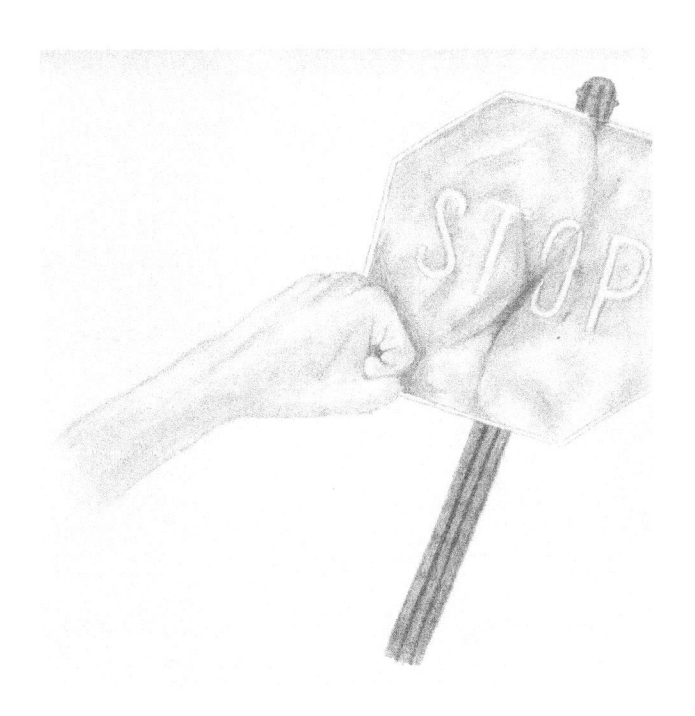

"Don't let the stigma of having a mental illness stop you from doing what's best for you!"

Gemma Gilfoyle

Smashing Through your Fear of Stigma

Have you ever lived inside your own head for so long you don't know who to trust, who to believe or what's even real?

If you answered yes, then I am with you on that. If you answered no, please be grateful you haven't. I can honestly say living in this mentally unstable world every day and feeling the way I do, is not nice.

I can say this c'os I have lived like this for many years. In fact, I have lived this way since I was a child. Unfortunately, this is quite possibly going to be my life, but I won't let that stop me. I know I have the most utter strength and ability to live a happier, healthier lifestyle. Even if it does mean having bouts of periods where I am low.

The thing is, having the right tools in place is huge, and sometimes those tools will change as you change and that's ok. If you're getting worse, it just means there are things that are unresolved and therefore you need to address past issues/trauma.

Facts about mental ill health

The term 'mental health' refers to the ability to function with daily life. Having a good positive sense of who you are, having the ability to deal with everyday stress, participate in society, think clearly and solve problems, and to make sense of the world around us.

Mental ill health is basically having the absence of some or all of these positive factors continuously throughout the day, weeks, months or even years.

<u>Did you know ….</u> 970 million people worldwide have a mental health or substance abuse disorder? (Our World in Data, 2018). Yes, you read that right. Do you still feel alone? You may do if you don't know any person who has mental ill health, or you may do if you don't have anyone to talk to. The chance of someone close to you not having/had mental illness at some point is slim but the stigma around mental ill health, makes people not want to speak up about dealing with these issues.

The World Health Organisation (WHO) define mental health as: "a state of wellbeing in which the individual realises his or her own abilities, can cope with the normal stresses of life, can work productively and fruitfully, and is able to make a contribution to his or her community".

Growing up with mental ill health and not knowing anything about it, only that people get locked up for being mentally ill, really took a lot out of me and I struggled so much for more years than I care to think about. Why? Because when we are programmed to believe something, it can really take a long time to break that stigma. The truth is - many more people are affected by mental ill health than you realise.

DID YOU KNOW: <u>1 in 4 people are diagnosed with mental ill health, while 1 in 5 report experiencing mental health issues but are not ever diagnosed?</u>

To me that is shocking, because mental ill health is all round us, yet the stigma is still there. Now don't get me wrong, the stigma has changed over the years but there is still an unhealthy stigma around mental ill health. I have spoken to many people who still don't realise they won't have their kids taken away for asking for help.

When it comes to stigma, men's mental health is really overlooked and it's really scary. People forget mental ill health does not discriminate because it doesn't matter who you are, what your race, religion, gender, or sexuality is. What if I told you suicide is higher in men than women how shocked would you be?

<u>5 DID YOU KNOW FACTS…</u>
1. Men make up the vast majority of the prison population. There are high rates of mental health problems and increasing rates of self-harm in prisons.
2. Three times as many men as women die by suicide.
3. Men aged 40-49 have the highest suicide rates in the UK
4. Nearly three-quarters of adults who go missing are men.
5. 87% of rough sleepers are men.
(Mentalhealth.org.uk)

I won't claim to know a lot about men's mental ill health, because firstly I am a woman and I don't fully get a man's struggle, and secondly, I have not done enough research. I have researched enough to know that while our men are struggling, they are staying silent. As a woman who suffers with mental ill health these facts within our men actually worry me.

Why mental ill health

So, you're probably asking why mental health and why I chose to be different with my chapter? Why I chose to do a lot of fact around mental health before I chose to tell you about me?....

Well, that's simple and comes with many reasons. The biggest two were the starting point of my downward spiral of mental ill health.

Growing up I always felt different. I always enjoyed being on my own more than being around others. I spent hours, if not days sometimes with my head in books, no interaction with people other than what was needed. When I got to my last year in primary school, I started getting bullied.

As I went into high school, I was attacked by the same guy and his friend in the school grounds. I will always be thankful to the 3 lads that came to help me out and stopped me from getting a real beating. They helped me to believe that there are good men out there. The bullying continued through our school after that, to the point where at the age of 14yrs, I stopped going to school, as in their eyes I was fine, and I did not need to move schools so I turned up when I could be bothered. Not long after, I was jumped by the two guys.

The second reason was that I lost my grandad to terminal cancer. Now, while it's natural to have a member of your family pass on, what's not natural is finding your grandad dying in his bed. While I have always been someone who is very much happy in her own bubble, watching my grandad being pulled out of his bed at the age of 11 to be resuscitated, was way too hard to deal with.

That day is something I struggle to remember, but I was kept off school because I was ill, but the weird thing is no one remembers me being ill. I just know that the whole morning felt really strange. Something did not feel right, and I remember feeling really concerned all morning. My mum went to her first job of the day. I received a phone call from my mum's friend, and I just remember I got this awful feeling and broke down to her. I started to shake, my breathing became shallow, and I started panicking telling my mum's friend something was wrong with my grandad as he was in bed and not up.

They could not understand my panic, and neither could I. I just knew something bad was happening and I needed help for my grandad. They asked me to go check and just wake him up although I knew it was not going to happen. I placed the house phone on the side and went to his room. I touched my grandad and he felt cold and had really shallow breathing (known as Cheyne-stokes breathing). Returning to the phone I was in full panic mode screaming "he won't wake up; he won't wake up" … "he is breathing funny". Lucky for me, my mum's friend and her husband lived a few doors away and they came to the house to help me.

They ran straight upstairs to my grandad's bedroom, and I instantly followed. The husband started talking to my grandad and heard his breathing and instantly everything changed. I don't know who rang for the ambulance or how I was removed from the situation at all. That part of my memory is gone. I just remember my grandad being pulled off the bed and the husband doing compressions on my Grandad. Next thing I knew I was walking down the road to the friend's house and my mum was walking up to the house panicking. After that I don't remember anything - even the day's following it.

From there on in, I knew I could not ask my mum for help. She had cared for her dad for years and now she had gone to work, left her daughter home whilst he was having a lie in. One which he had never done before – ever! And he had passed away in her home whilst her daughter was watching. I have no understanding of what guilt she may have felt, and it has never been talked about since, even after all these years, simply because I can't.

Watching my grandad struggle to breathe on the landing that day, was the first time I was able to block out anything that came at me. Any trauma that has happened in my life since then, I have been able to detach myself from that situation. So, although I know it's happened, I feel numb to it which means I don't ever deal with the issue at hand.

This is just a small snippet into my life, but it's also where my mental ill heath started and since then things have just gotten worse. Many things happen in my life which have led me to live a life where I stopped asking for help. I always suffered in silence… because whenever I had asked for help, I was laughed at and told I didn't need it or made to believe it was my own fault and therefore, I had to just get over it myself.

Not asking for help has led me to self-harm and to live a life with suicidal thoughts, ptsd, depression, anxiety, social anxiety and more recently a diagnosis of a binge-eating disorder. The thoughts that go through my head are daily torture. The thoughts in my head are what have been said to me over & over for many years by people who I thought loved me. I feel like my brain just does not seem to absorb any positivity, which means I never felt good enough for anyone. I felt like me walking this planet was doing more harm than good and I was pushing everyone away so I would never have to get hurt.

With no one helping me, I decided to start helping myself and I have learned 5 techniques that really saved me. Now, these are so simple yet have made a huge difference and I want to share them with you.

If you have such severe depression, then these still may not work fully, but they will make a huge difference as they did for me. And while I am not fully better, they keep me going.

<u>The 5 technique's I use - Create a morning routine and a sleep routine, Use deep breathing, Keep a mood journal, and meditate.</u>

Having a routine in the morning and a sleep routine will help you start and finish your day right. That includes making your bed - that way you have always achieved something. Use deep breathing when you start getting anxious or stressed - it helps slow the body down. Mood journals are great to keep track of where your head is at. Write everything down from good to bad - you may even find your triggers and definitely find 5 mins in a day to meditate. Sit and be at one with yourself using deep breaths - you will feel so much more content with yourself after.

You see, life is a struggle at the best of times, especially when you're battling with mental illness, and it feels impossible. Every day, daily tasks, even getting up, all feel like an effort. It feels like you can never break out of the darkness that has set in your head.

If you take anything from this chapter, then just know it is possible to live with mental ill health. It is possible to get better and it is ok to do things differently. Not everything one person does, will work for you and that's ok. You must be willing to fight til you find what is right. Mental ill health is not an easy journey to walk but I fully believe only the strongest are given the chance to walk it. I want you to know you're never alone on this journey. There is always someone starting it and plenty more dealing with it. All you have to do is reach out and ask.

DON'T LET THE STIGMA OF HAVING A MENTAL ILLNESS STOP YOU FROM DOING WHAT'S BEST FOR YOU.
YOU DESERVE TO LIVE YOUR LIFE AND BE HAPPY... KNOW YOUR WORTH!

DEDICATION

In loving memory of my grandad Edward Martin Jones – Losing you was one of the hardest things I have ever had to deal with and while it may have been the start of a lot of issues in my life, I can't ever be without those issues, as I would never have been able to protect my boys and help people the way I am doing right now.
Grandad, I will love you – always and forever!

Gemma Gilfoyle

Gemma Gilfoyle is a Life Coach, Entrepreneur, #1 International Best-selling co-author, Speaker and Influencer. She has 6+ years in business and is all about MOTIVATING EMPOWERING and UPLIFTING people by getting them to step into their POWER. Gemma has suffered from mental health for many years. Yet she has not let that define who she is and has used her knowledge and strength to create her own business, so she can help other people do the same.

Gemma grew up as the 2nd child in her family and always felt different. She lived most of her childhood with her head in novels, knowing there was more to life than your average 9-5. Becoming a teen mum at 17, Gemma jumped straight into work and didn't think about anything else, she had lost herself in the rat race of work. Her workdays had gotten so long that at times she was known to have worked 18hours shift.

Diving back into books and finding out she was pregnant, Gemma took time out to rediscover herself. Her past work had always been supporting and helping people. Having managed to gain full control of her own mental health, along with her passion for helping others, meant it took no time in finding her true calling as a life coach.

Gemma is a unique individual whose passion and love for helping others makes her stand out from other people. She wears her heart on her sleeve and will always go that one step further for her clients.

WEBLINKS:

Website: https://www.gemmagilfoyle.com/
Instagram: https://www.instagram.com/gemmalgilfoyle/
Facebook: https://www.facebook.com/gemmalgilfoyle/
Pinterest: https://www.pinterest.co.uk/gemmagilfoyle/
Podcast: https://anchor.fm/gemma-gilfoyle

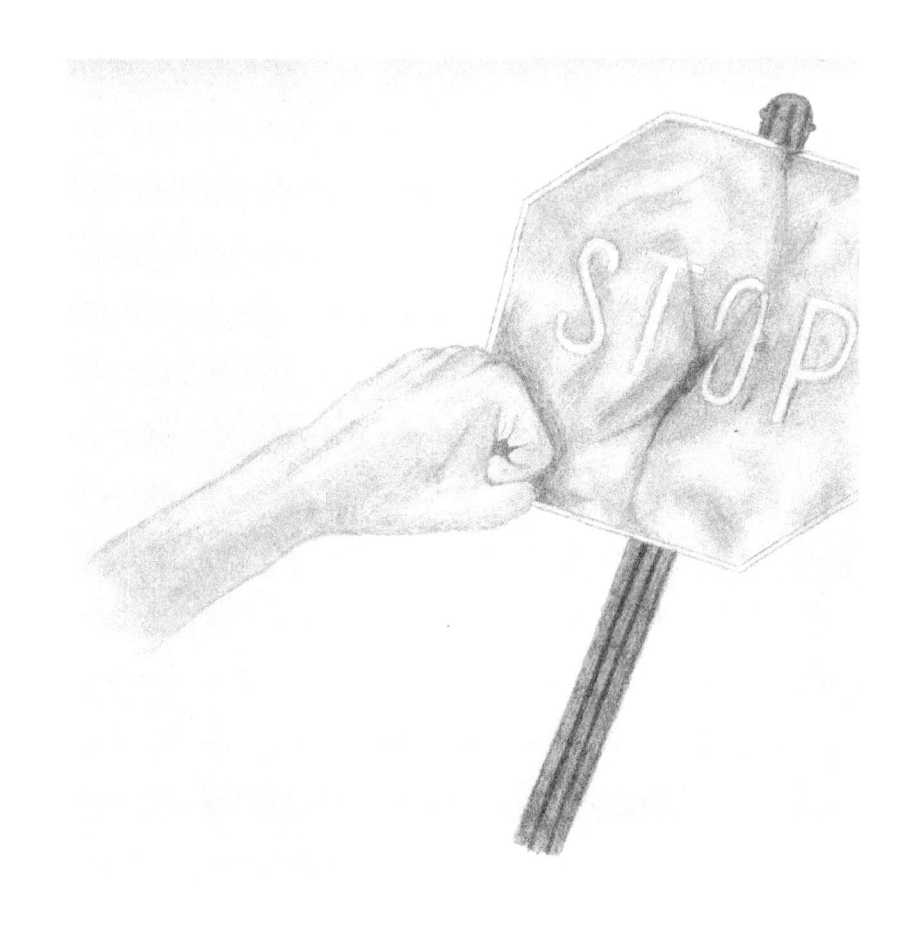

Closing Thoughts

As I write the closing thoughts of this book, to end the trilogy, that is the "Smashing Through…" series, I must say it's been a journey and a complete honour to bring all these incredible chapters of the inspiring co-author's real lives into fruition.

I am dedicated in all areas of my life to be real and raw, genuine, and true and to bring the respect and empathy into my work. I get complete joy from it all and I'm so humbled and privileged to do what I do, and I love it.

In your life, you will experience both ups and downs. It's like watching the heartbeat monitor. What you do need to know is that you can take each 5 minutes as it is, breathe deeply and focus on your determination to move forward, a little at a time, through anything and everything that you are going through.

Reach out to your support network, and if you don't have one (and even if you do), please connect with the co-authors in the "Smashing Through…" series, as we are all here for you.

Life can sometimes feel like a daily grind, however, when you focus on gratitude and be thankful for the smallest of things, you can truly feel and be blessed for the health, money, people, opportunities, and experiences in your life and much more. The list is endless.

You are worthy of goodness and greatness. When you can find a positive outlook on something, then I encourage you to hold onto that with both hands and cherish every single moment you have. Life is precious and meaningful when you decide it to be.

I am sending you lots of love, happiness, and joy into your life. Remember you're worth more than rubies and diamonds.

Rebecca.x

Acknowledgements of the "SMASHING THROUGH' Series

Firstly, I'd like to acknowledge and give thanks to you, the reader. I appreciate you immensely and hope you are inspired by every co-author who has shared a layer of their life-changing experience with you through these pages. Thank you for the wonderful reviews we have received and all your lovely feedback. It means so much. Please use the hashtags below when sharing on social media). Thank you so much.

Secondly, I'd like to acknowledge all the co-authors from each of the books. You were brave and courageous to write your story and I am very humbled and proud of you. They are:

SMASHING THROUGH THE GLASS CEILING (#STTGC)
Alison Parsons, Ray Coates, Andy Ashworth, Angie Candler, Sherry Cannon-Jones, Aneska Vermaak, Jilly Ashworth, Louise Grant, Rachel Allaston, Julie Dickens, Lisa Lowndes, Imani Speaks and Timothy Parent.

SMASHING THROUGH THE BRICK WALL (#STTBW)
Carole Arnold, Maria Harris, Imani Speaks, Natalie Allanson, Chevala Hardy, Lakeisha McGee, Caroline Brown, Lorraine Ford, Michelle Roche, Louisa Moulton and Michelle Netherton.

SMASHING THROUGH THE STOP SIGN OF LIFE (#STTSSOL)
Phoebe Adams, Gemma Gilfoyle, Maria Harris, Susan Anne Lynn, Louise McGough, Julie Dickens, Victoria Sainsbury-Brown, Mandy Vermaak, Karlene Jordan, Ray Coates, Michelle Roche, Louise Adair, Sherri Olsen, Ashley Stanford, Michelle Netherton and Sherry Cannon-Jones.

Next, I'd like to say a big thank you to Irene Pro for all the amazing and incredible work that you do. It's been an honour to work with you on some fabulous projects and I am so blessed to have you in my life, both personally and professionally. You are a remarkable lady and I'm so full of gratitude for you.

Thank you so much to Shani Rogers & Maria Harris for the brainstorming and assisting me with titling this amazing book, "Smashing Through The Stop Sign of Life". I appreciate you both.

I would also like to acknowledge my daughter Phoebe Adams as the illustrator for all 3 books of this series. You have an outstanding talent and you've completed some awesome work. Thank you so much.

And, also Irene Pro, Jenny Ford, and Imani Speaks for the Forewords in each of the books. You truly are incredible human beings. Gratitude.

I would also like to thank the universe and all of her wisdom, with divine downloads to me with my vision as we have 3 exceptional books that will empower and inspire many people who read them. They are part of a huge legacy, of which I am deeply proud.

I'd like to say thank you to my dear friend Fiona Dennis, who is the most phenomenal and extraordinary lady I have ever met. I'm so full of gratitude for you being in my life and I appreciate you immensely.

Thank you to my son Dominic Adams. You have helped shape me into the parent and person I am today with your special needs. I appreciate you and so grateful to have you as my son. I am so proud of your accomplishments so far and know that you are a joy.

Finally, I want to acknowledge and give my thanks to my beautiful Mum, Carole Arnold. You have been a tower of strength throughout my entire life, a role model to many and an incredible parent to me. I was and still am blessed to call you my Mum and know that I am so proud of all that you accomplished whilst you were here on this amazing planet.

I miss you dearly and I know that, even though you didn't get to see your own chapter in print, you were very proud of the books, and everyone involved in them too.
I love you Mum and always will. Be at peace and rest in love.

Rebecca Adams.x

Smashing Through the Glass Ceiling!

True stories of abuse, tragedy and heartache leading to strength, hope and happiness.

Compiled by Rebecca Adams
4X's International Best Selling Author

Smashing Through The Glass Ceiling is a Compilation of 14 International Authors sharing their personal, powerful, life-changing stories

Available on Amazon

Available on Amazon

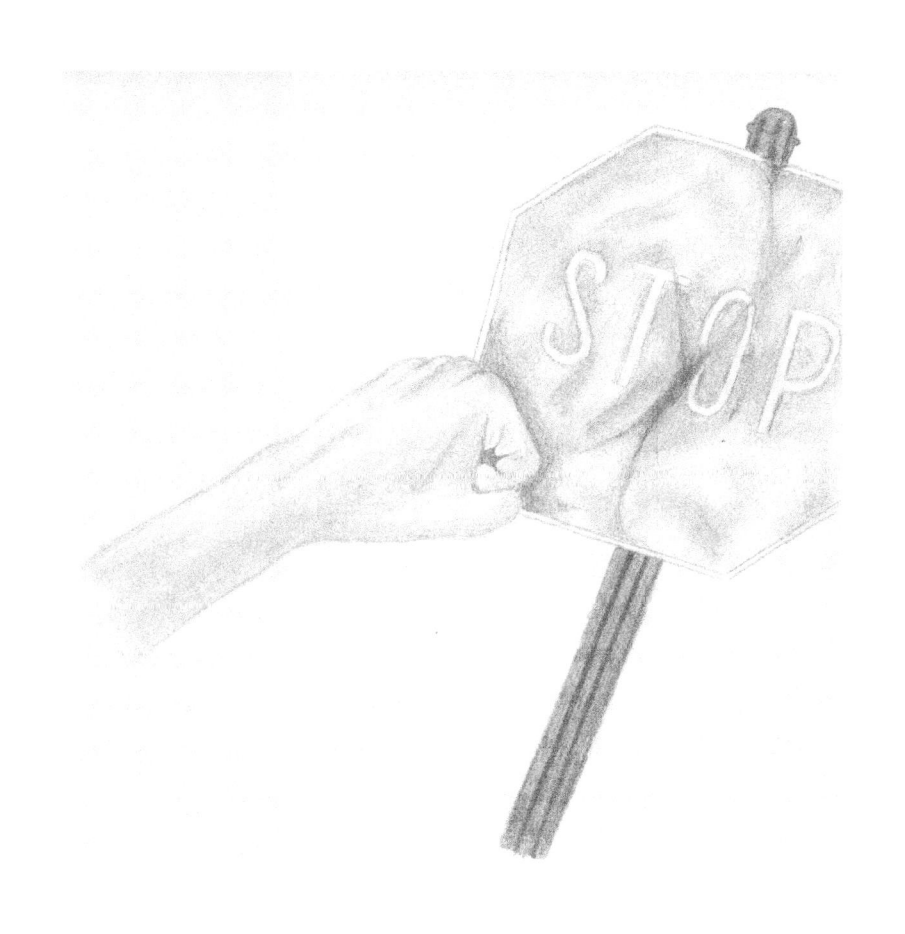

Book Sponsors

FEEL ALIVE AND LIVE A PHENOMENAL LIFE™

Rebecca offers a huge range of opportunities to work with her to empower yourself with all areas of your life and business through her online digital programs, private bespoke coaching and much more.

Rebecca loves to share her highly positive energy with as many people around the world and if you stay with her long enough, she'll inspire and motivate you and empower your mindset so you know that you can achieve anything.

Available at all different price points you can tap into Rebecca's work at whatever level you are at too. Connect with her on her website below.

Rebecca Adams

www.rebeccaadamsbiz.com

Smashing Through The Stop Sign Of Life

Little Ruby's Treats Expertise

IT Help and Advice Coaching
Website Builds & ReVamps
IT Blogs and Guest Blogs
Maria's Books
Logo Creation

The whole process of Little Ruby's Treats has been to build a solid foundation for all things "Treats". The Business is there to make the customers and clients feel Special, enable them to expand their knowledge and feel more confident in their work and passions.

My Business is split into 2 sections Little Ruby's Treats – Printing Service and Little Ruby's Treats – Expertise.

My Expertise side of things is there to allow the customer/client to expand their business in a way that suits them and to make sure they can feel special and like they have Treated themselves and their Business also.

So, if you're reading this advert and want to expand your knowledge and feel more confident in your business and yourself, please come and check out Little Ruby's Treats on our website at www.littlerubystreats.co.uk

I look forward in helping you grow and be more confident and more knowledgeable soon

Maria's IT Help and Advice Blog

www.littlerubystreats.co.uk

love
Maria

www.littlerubystreats.co.uk

1 on 1 IT Help and Advice Coaching!

Bundle Sessions and Hourly Rates

5 Sessions (1 hour) - £140
10 sessions (1 hour) - £280
5 sessions (2 hours) - £280
10 sessions (2 hours) - £560

Hourly rates
on your choice of Subject

Connect with me today
to discuss your needs

Maria's Web Design/Logo Packages

Full Builds, Revamps and Logo Creations

Full Website Build - £400
Revamp Build - £250
Logos - £50

Connect with me today
to discuss your needs

Imani Speaks Show & Podcast Imani Speaks – Stop the World I Want to Get Off brings you interviews and conversations with talented musician, authors, thought leaders, transformational coaches, business coaches and other community angels who are making a difference locally and globally.

Imani Speaks
Radio Presenter/DJ & Podcaster
www.conciousradio.com
Mondays 6-8pm
Podcast
Stop The World I want to get off for an Hour

Imani is a Life, Love & Wellbeing coach; providing non-judgemental sacred conversational space for clients to unpack painful past emotional energy. Imani helps people release their emotional clutter, freeing up space for them to discover their soul's goals.

Free (one hour) experiential session available.

Life, Love & Wellbeing Coach

www.imanispeaks.com
www.imanispeaksmondays@gmail.com

12 Weeks
SOUL CENTRED JOY FOR LIFE

This 1:1 counselling program is for women who are feeling stuck & trapped in their own lives, who are experiencing darkness, continually 'just existing', not living far less thriving. Women who have lost their identity & sense of self.

Your life feels out of control, you are controlled by others, feel invisible & make poor choices resulting in you always feeling unfulfilled. You don't experience joy & abundance. Negativity, numbness, apathy, no direction & purpose have started to filter into all areas of your life - from your own well-being to family, friendships & work/career. It's no longer just you that's suffering - your relationships are too. You don't know who you are anymore but one thing you do know is that you don't like who you have become.

You want to feel like you used to, your inner voice says there's definitely more to life - problem is you just don't know what it is anymore! You don't have to feel like this!

Follow my guide, break free & find freedom. Live a life of soul centred joy, love, peace, & fulfilment in everything you choose to do - then let this cause a ripple effect & make a difference to the world around you. Rediscover & rebuild your identity & sense of self. Really connect with the woman within, your soul, your authentic self.

The program covers: reality check, clarity, habits, repeating patterns, daily routines, affirmations, gratitude, mindfulness, beliefs, behaviours, blockages, fears, core values, your authenticity/uniqueness, vision & action plans.

Light up YOUR PASSION FOR LIFE again. Feel energised, empowered, motivated, optimistic & confident but most importantly content. Feel joyful, abundant & fulfilled! A truly transformational self-development & growth program!

www.sherrycannonjones.com

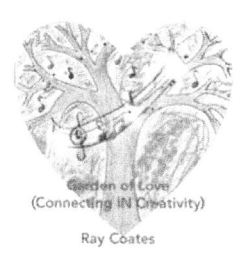

Ray Coates

An INCREDIBLE album of Creative Connection 'Garden of Love (Connecting IN Creativity)', includes global collaborations from Australia; Canada; USA and the UK.

Described by guitarist and record producer Mark Walker as: '10 bands in 1 album', 'Garden of Love (Connecting IN Creativity)' is available on CD NOW for £14.99 (not including postage outside of the uk).

The album is also available on all digital download/streaming platforms including iTunes http://itunes.apple.com/album/id1576506329?ls=1&app=itunes

Let your ears hear the sounds of unity; love; joy; hope; unconditional love; gratitude; determination; life; humility; respect and freedom, contained IN the 'Garden of Love'. 'Garden of Love (Connecting IN Creativity)'

Includes 3 collaborations with authors in this book 'Smashing Through the Stop Sign of Life'...

Track 7 'Keep Going Always', inspired by the phenomenal 'Smashing Through' series book compiler and International best selling author Rebecca Adams.

Track 9 'Be Like This Child' co-lyrics written by the amazing Susan Anne Lynn

Track 11 'Altered State' co-lyrics provided by the incredible Michelle Roche.

www.raycoatesvoice.com

Thank You

Thank you so much for purchasing and choosing our collaboration book "Smashing Through The Stop Sign of Life". The incredible journey of collaborating with men and women co-authors both in the UK and internationally has been an honour, both personally and professionally. Together we all share mutual empathy and deep understanding of our true life-changing experiences of mental health, dreams, shocks, cancer and hurdles leading to strength, power and positivity.

I'd like to personally thank every co-author for putting their trust and faith in me directing this remarkable project and collectively making our voices heard!

Rebecca Adams

Printed in Great Britain
by Amazon